Revolutionary Citizens

AFRICAN AMERICANS
1776–1804

The Black Regiment.1778   The Battle of Rhode Island

THE YOUNG OXFORD HISTORY OF
**AFRICAN
AMERICANS**

Robin D. G. Kelley and Earl Lewis
General Editors

Revolutionary Citizens

❖ ❖ ❖

AFRICAN AMERICANS
1776-1804

DANIEL C. LITTLEFIELD

Oxford University Press
New York • Oxford

For Valinda

Oxford University Press

Oxford   New York
Athens Auckland Bangkok Bogotá Bombay
Buenos Aires Calcutta Cape Town Dar es Salaam Delhi
Florence Hong Kong Istanbul Karachi
Kuala Lumpur Madras Madrid Melbourne
Mexico City Nairobi Paris Singapore
Taipei Tokyo Toronto
and associated companies in
Berlin Ibadan

Library of Congress Cataloging-in-Publication Data
Littlefield, Daniel C.
Revolutionary Citizens: African Americans 1776–1804 / by Daniel C. Littlefield.
p. cm. — (The young Oxford history of African Americans: v. 3)
Includes bibliographical references and index.
ISBN 0-19-508715-1 (library ed.); ISBN 0-19-508502-7 (series, library ed.)
1. Afro-Americans—History—To 1863—Juvenile literature.
2. United States—History—Revolution, 1775–1783—
Afro-Americans—Juvenile literature.
3. United States—History—1783–1815—Juvenile literature.
[1. Afro-Americans—History—To 1863. 2. United States—History—Revolution, 1775–
1783. 3. United States—History—1783–1815.]
I. Title. II. Series.
E185.18.L58   1997
973'.0496073—dc20   96-8470
CIP

1 3 5 7 9 8 6 4 2

Printed in the United States of America
on acid-free paper

Design: Sandy Kaufman
Layout: Loraine Machlin
Picture research: Lisa Kirchner, Laura Kreiss

On the cover: Detail from *The Death of General Warren at the Battle of Bunker's Hill,
17 June 1775* by John Trumbull
Frontispiece: A black soldier from the First Rhode Island Regiment
Page 9: Detail from *The Contribution of the Negro to Democracy in America*, (1943) by
Charles White, 11'9" x 17'3". Hampton University Museum, Hampton, Virginia

CONTENTS

ROBIN D. G. KELLEY
EARL LEWIS

INTRODUCTION

◇ ◇ ◇

In the 150 years since African slaves' forced arrival in the 17th century, little exposed the contradictions between slavery and freedom for Africans as much as this nation's fight for independence from Great Britain. It was a contradiction many people resolved to settle. Some, such as the patriot Crispus Attucks, joined with other colonists in striking direct blows for liberty. Others, meanwhile, heard the pleas for loyalty to the British crown, and with the promise of emancipation as their reward, remained faithful to the old order only to see it vanish before them. But whether in the poems of Phillis Wheatley, the legal action of freed slave Quok Walker, or the efforts of businessman Paul Cuffe, Americans of African descent helped define what it meant to be revolutionary citizens.

In fact, as the clamor for independence from Great Britain intensified, so too did the debate over slavery. Many who participated in the debate recognized that slavery remained a central form of labor in both the North and the South. Although it was a minority view, some American colonists favored emancipation. They pointed to the success of the few blacks who managed to purchase their freedom and gain an economic foothold before the 1760s. But in a land where dark skin signaled a lower social position, the few blacks who lived free represented the exception. For the enslaved, independence was not a philosophical debate. It was an alternative to permanent bondage.

As a result, African Americans took a keen interest in public affairs. A small group of Africans in Massachusetts, for example, petitioned the provisional House of Representatives for their freedom as early as 1773. Such petitions increased in frequency after the Declaration of Independence. Others acted individually, suing their masters for their freedom and thereby insisting that they were citizens with the right to seek redress. And after five generations on North American soil, the promise of

A list of the free blacks who fought for the First Rhode Island Regiment. New England blacks were involved early on in the revolutionary struggle.

freedom seemed tantalizingly close, so a few clung to the potential for British citizenship, trading loyalty to the crown for freedom. No matter which side they supported, African people saw in the war an opportunity to escape slavery.

The revolutionary era, however, did more than accelerate the push for freedom. It also saw the birth of a people called African Americans. In the crucible of the United States' birth, Africans claimed they too were Americans. They emphasized the role they played in building the infant nation and in securing its freedom. From their embrace of the religious awakening to the formation of independent institutions, they inserted themselves into the social and cultural life of the country. Ever aware of the implication of freedom, they spread word of their own efforts throughout the Americas, and took pleasure as other African peoples liberated themselves in Haiti.

This volume closely examines the men and women of African origin who came of age during the era of the American Revolution, showing their words, their deeds, and their triumphs and defeats. It demonstrates the inextricable link between slavery and freedom, and African Americans and the promise and reality of democracy. It is a poignant story peopled by those who fancied themselves revolutionary citizens.

This book is part of an 11-volume series that narrates African-American history from the 15th through the 20th centuries. Since the 1960s, a rapid explosion in research on black Americans has significantly modified previous understanding of that experience. Studies of slavery, African-American culture, social protest, families, and religion, for example, silenced those who had previously labeled black Americans insignificant historical actors. This new research followed a general upsurge of interest in the social and cultural experiences of the supposedly powerless men and women who did not control the visible reins of power. The result has been a careful and illuminating portrait of how ordinary people make history and serve as the architects of their own destinies.

This series explores many aspects of the lives of African Americans. It describes how blacks shaped and changed the history of this nation. It also places the lives of African Americans in the context of the Americas as a whole. We start the story more than a century before the day in 1619 when 19 "negars" stepped off a Spanish ship in Jamestown, Virginia, and end with the relationship between West Indian immigrants and African Americans in large urban centers like New York in the late 20th century.

At the same time, the series addresses a number of interrelated questions: What was life like for the first Africans to land in the Americas, and what were the implications for future African Americans? Were all Africans and African Americans enslaved? How did race shape slavery and how did slavery influence racism? The series also considers questions about male-female relationships, the forging of African-American communities, religious beliefs and practices, the experiences of the young, and the changing nature of social protest. The key events in American history are here, too, but viewed from the perspective of African Americans. The result is a fascinating and compelling story of nearly five centuries of African-American history.

THE YOUNG OXFORD HISTORY OF
AFRICAN AMERICANS

PREFACE

◇ ◇ ◇

Perhaps no people in the world more keenly awaited and appreciated the changes that swept America and Europe during the Age of Revolution than African Americans. They were a people largely enslaved and forced to labor for others. Even when free, they were normally excluded from full participation in society and politics. And so they readily understood the true meaning of the ringing declarations that proclaimed all people to be created free and equal. No group knew better what it meant to be taxed without their consent; for their tax was not merely on a portion of their goods but was a taking of their all. One of their most important roles during this period was to make European Americans see the error of their ways and live up to the best of their promise. In that, they had only partial success.

This book considers the changes wrought in African-American life primarily in the United States, but it touches on much more than that. For the ripples set off when British colonists in North America rejected their mother country had international effects. It created waves that carried African-American settlers to England, Canada, Africa, and the West Indies. Moreover, the fight against slavery and the slave trade were also linked. In other words, African Americans in the United States were not isolated from international events; politics and personalities in England,

> FIVE POUNDS REWARD.
>
> RUN-AWAY from the sub-scriber, a negro fellow named DANIEL, thirty-three years of age, a low well set fellow, has a very flat nose, down look, black complexion, and but few words in common, he can read some in print, and is a black-smith, silver-smith and a cooper; carried away with him silver-smiths tools, and different suits of homespun cloths, one pair of buck-skin breeches, and one Dutch blanket. Any person that will deliver him to me, or secure said negro so that I may get him again, shall receive the above reward from
>
> ABRAHAM TAYLOR.
> Bertie County, March 24, 1791.

Daniel, a slave belonging to a North Carolina man, ran away from his master in 1791. A five pound reward was offered for his return.

On June 5, 1783,
George Washington,
the commander in
chief of the Continen-
tal army, personally
signed the discharge
papers for Oliver
Cromwell, a black
man who served for
six years with the
Jersey Battalion.

By His Excellency
GEORGE WASHINGTON, Esq;
General and Commander in Chief of the Forces of the United States of America.

THESE are to CERTIFY that the Bearer hereof *Oliver Cromwell Private* in the *Jersey Battalion* ~~Regiment~~, having faithfully served the United States *for Six Years* _____ and being inlisted for the War only, is hereby DISCHARGED from the American Army.

GIVEN at HEAD-QUARTERS the *fifth* day *June 1783*

G Washington

France, and Haiti influenced what happened in the United States and vice versa. In this regard, few events were more important than the revolution and movement for independence in Haiti.

Finally, we will look at changes in the lives and culture of African Americans that resulted from revolution in the United States and the ways that European Americans justified their continued repression of their black compatriots. During this period British North America changed from a society in which a small group of wealthy white men had almost complete control over all political and economic decisions to one in which the principles of democracy and equality began to level the access to power. This was a change for the better, even though, from an African-American point of view, the society was still flawed. It is a story of struggle, of victory and setback. It is a story worth knowing.

PHILLIS WHEATLEY, NEGRO SERVANT to Mr JOHN WHEATLEY, of BOSTON.

Published according to Act of Parliament, Septr 1, 1773 by Arch.^d Bell,

Bookseller N.º 8 near the Saracens Head Aldgate.

CHAPTER 1

PHILLIS WHEATLEY AND THE RIGHTS OF MAN

◇ ◇ ◇

In October 1772 a young Boston woman wrote a poem dedicated to William Legge, earl of Dartmouth, who lived in London. A man reputedly of humane character, the earl had recently been appointed by the British king as secretary of state for the colonies. He took charge at a troubled period in relations between Britain and its North American possessions. Since the end of the French and Indian War in 1763, the colonists had become discontented because of new British policies about taxation and restrictions on trade. The young Boston woman hoped that the earl would respond favorably to the difficult issues that prevented harmony between the king and his colonial subjects. She flattered him as a friend of "Fair *Freedom*" who would end the "hated *faction*," or dissension, that the crisis created.

Ironically, the young woman who wrote so knowledgeably about the colonial struggle for liberty and who was so aware of the political affairs and personalities of the day was not free herself. Her bondage gave her an acute sensitivity to issues of slavery and freedom. As she wrote the earl:

> Should you, my lord, while you peruse my song,
> Wonder from whence *my love of Freedom sprung*,
> I, young in life, by *seeming cruel fate*
> Was snatched from Afric's fancy'd happy seat;
> Such, such my case. And can I then but pray
> Others may never feel *tyrannic sway*?

The poet's name was Phillis Wheatley, and she was brought from the West Coast of Africa, probably from the Senegambia region, to Boston, Massachusetts, in 1761. Her life spanned the era of America's revolutionary struggle with Great Britain, and her death in 1784 followed by one year Britain's recognition of America's independence. She wrote a poem lauding George Washington as well as one praising King George III, and she attracted the attention of revolutionary patriots such as Benjamin Franklin, Thomas Jefferson, Thomas Paine, John Hancock, and the American naval hero John Paul Jones. She was the first African American to publish a book of poetry and she gained international notice. Yet she was also a slave and composed most of her poetry while in that condition. Her color, enslavement, keen intelligence, and, quite likely, her gender all contributed to her fame. She was seen as unique because many people at that time did not think that Africans had intelligence or capability equal to that of Europeans. Many believed that Africans could not be educated, that they had no capacity for original or creative thought, and that they were best suited to servitude.

Phillis Wheatley began early on to disprove these notions. She was only seven or eight years old when she landed in Boston, but as John Wheatley, her purchaser, related, "Without any Assistance from School Education, and by only what she was taught in the Family, she, in sixteen Months Time from her Arrival, attained the English Language, to which she was an utter Stranger before, to such a Degree, as to read any, the most difficult Parts of the Sacred Writings, to the great Astonishment of all who heard her." Doubtless her owners quickly saw a chance to test the proposition that Africans were unable to learn and encouraged her to persist in educating herself. John Wheatley bought Phillis to aid his wife Susannah, whom friends described as a woman of unusual refinement, sensitivity, and religiosity. She also had an interest in missionary activity, particularly among Africans and Native Americans. These characteristics help explain why Susannah encouraged Phillis to get an education. Besides studying Latin and English classics, she was tutored in astronomy, ancient and modern geography, and history. When one considers that she was a slave and also a woman in a period when most women and even more slaves received no such attention, her situation and accomplishments are remarkable. She was almost certainly one of the most highly educated young women in Boston at the time.

An Address to the Atheist, By P. Wheatley at the age of
14 years. — 1767. —

Muse! where shall I begin the spacious field
To tell what curses unbelief doth yield?
Thou who dost daily feel his hand, and rod
Darest thou deny the Essence of a God!
If there's no heav'n, ah! whither wilt thou go
Make thy Elysium in the shades below?
If there's no God from whom did all things spring
He made the greatest and minutest thing
Angelic ranks no less his Power display
Than the least mite scarce visible to day
With vast astonishment my soul is struck
Have Reas'ning powers thy dark breast forsook?
The Laws deep Graven by the hand of God,
Seal'd with Immanuel's all-redeeming blood:
This second point thy folly dares deny
On thy devoted head for vengeance cry—
Turn then I pray thee from the dangerous road
Rise from the dust and seek the mighty God.
His is bright truth without a dark disguise
And his are wisdom's all beholding eyes
With labour'd snares our Adversary great
Withholds from us the Kingdom and the seat
Bliss weeping waits thee, in her arms to fly
To thir own regions of felicity —
Perhaps thy ignorance will ask us where?
Go to the corner stone he will declare.
Thy heart in unbelief will harden'd grow
Tho' much indulg'd in vicious pleasure now —
Thou tak'st unusual means; the path forbear
Unkind to others to thy self severe—
Methinks I see the consequence thou'rt blind
Thy unbelief disturbs the peaceful Mind.

Phillis Wheatley wrote this poem, "An Address to the Atheist," when she was only 14 years old.

She was also well connected, for her mistress encouraged her religious interests and introduced her to leading advocates of the 18th-century evangelical Christian movement in America and Britain. Evangelical religion has been described as more a feeling and an attitude about religion than a strict religious system. Evangelicals refused to be bound by the rules of formal church organizations. They placed great emphasis on a personal knowledge of the Bible, a direct and emotional experience of God's grace, and the unity and equality of those saved by faith in the Holy Spirit. Consequently, they weakened existing distinctions between masters and slaves and undercut the traditional Christian toleration of slavery. Though not all evangelicals opposed slavery, the most radical among them did, particularly those of the Baptist and Methodist denominations that began a rapid expansion in England and America during Phillis's lifetime. They directed a particular appeal to the slaves.

The English noblewoman Salina Hastings, countess of Huntingdon, friend of Susannah Wheatley, and patron of Phillis, was a supporter of evangelical Methodism. Her personal chaplain, George Whitefield (whom Phillis celebrated in an elegy), was the leading figure in a religious revival movement in America known as the Great Awakening (1739–45). It was characterized by highly emotional preaching, often delivered by itinerant, or roving, ministers who sometimes preached in fields or tents as well as in churches. It united black and white people in religious community and inspired some to reflect upon the blacks' secular (or earthly) condition, including speculations concerning their mental capabilities.

Phillis's achievements, therefore, had more than personal significance. She was embraced by abolitionists, many of whom were evangelicals, and offered as evidence that black people had the same possibilities as white people and deserved the same opportunities. After her *Poems on Various Subjects, Religious and Moral* was published in London in 1773, the Philadelphia physician and abolitionist Benjamin Rush extravagantly praised her "singular genius and accomplishments."

POEMS

ON

VARIOUS SUBJECTS,

RELIGIOUS AND MORAL.

BY

PHILLIS WHEATLEY,

NEGRO SERVANT to Mr. JOHN WHEATLEY, of BOSTON, in NEW ENGLAND.

Upon publication of her only volume of poetry in 1773, Wheatley was hailed both in America and in England for her talent. However, her fame was short-lived. She died in poverty in 1778.

European scientist John Friedrich Blumenbach likewise acclaimed her poems, calling them "a collection which scarcely any one who has any taste for poetry could read without pleasure." He spoke less about their quality, perhaps, than about the anomaly that anyone of her color and circumstances could produce poetry at all. London reviewers thought her book demonstrated a talent that made her continued servitude a disgrace and chided Bostonians for this inconsistency in the age of protest against British oppression.

Her book, dedicated to the countess of Huntingdon, was printed a year after the famous Somerset decision of 1772, a court case that placed severe limits on slavery in England and caused considerable unease for her young master, Mrs. Wheatley's son Nathaniel, when they traveled there together in the summer of 1773. At the center of the case was James Somerset, an American slave taken to London by his Boston master in 1769. In England, Somerset escaped, only to be recaptured and as punishment threatened with relocation to the more rigorous slave environment of Jamaica. His plight came to the attention of Granville Sharp, an abolitionist committed to ending slavery in Britain. Chief Justice Lord Mansfield, who heard the case, was reluctant to make the decision for liberty toward which he felt the law leaned, because he feared the reactions of colonial planters if all the servants they had brought to England were suddenly declared free. He also feared the social and economic consequences of freeing all the slaves. He therefore delayed and attempted to get the case dismissed. When this tactic failed, he ordered Somerset's master to release him from service and established the precedent that in Britain slaves could not be compelled to serve. Although this case did not actually end slavery in Great Britain, as historians so often maintain, it did make the atmosphere uncongenial for slaveholders. Moreover, it brought the issue of slavery before the public and excited much sympathy for the slaves. Phillis Wheatley, however, did not take advantage of the situation. Instead, she cut short her stay and returned to Boston when her mistress, then ailing, requested her presence.

Her popular success in Britain notwithstanding, not everyone was impressed by Phillis's accomplishments. Despite his stirring affirmation in the Declaration of Independence that all men were created equal, Thomas Jefferson had severe reservations about blacks' abilities. Moreover, he readily discounted whatever evidence he found that discredited his opinion. Consequently, he dismissed Phillis Wheatley as being incompetent as a poet. "The compositions published under her name," he said, "are below the dignity of criticism."

A Jamaica planter, Edward Long, was even more harsh. He intended to parody Wheatley's verse and the uses to which she had been put by abolitionists when he wrote:

> What woeful stuff this madrigal would be
> In some starv'd, hackney sonneteer, or me!
> But let a *Negroe* own the happy lines,
> How the wit brightens! How the Style refines!
> Before his sacred name flies ev'ry fault,
> And each exalted stanza teems with thought!

Long clearly intended to suggest that the merits of Wheatley's poetry derived solely from the fact that she was black. Yet he exhibited a certain

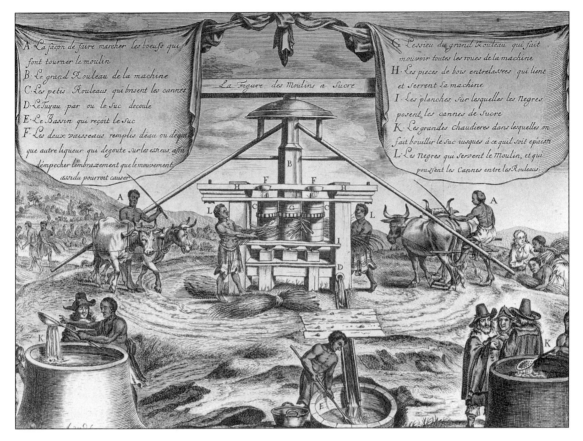

illogic because, while she may not have been, in his estimation, a genius, the common assertion was that blacks had not even a minimal competence.

The New World in which these commentators lived seemed to support such doubts, because by the middle of the 18th century, Africans were enslaved throughout the Americas. Bound African labor was associated primarily with sugar cultivation in Brazil and the Caribbean, the major plantation regions at the time. But slaves also grew coffee, cotton, rice, indigo, tobacco, and other crops in these areas and elsewhere. Additionally, Africans, slave and free, worked in mining and cattle raising in Spanish and Portuguese America, and they performed skilled and domestic chores in rural and urban locales (such as Phillis Wheatley's Boston). In British North America—the area that became the United States— colonials grew rice, supplemented with indigo after the 1760s, in coastal Georgia and South Carolina; primarily tobacco as a cash crop in the Chesapeake region of Virginia and Maryland; grain crops in the middle

Africans process sugarcane on a Caribbean plantation. Sugar required the most labor and was the most difficult New World crop to produce.

colonies of Delaware, Pennsylvania, New Jersey, and New York; and vegetables and dairy products in New England, where shipping was a major activity. Though Africans worked in practically all regions of North America, they were crucial to the economies of the colonies south of Pennsylvania.

Abolitionist sentiment began to develop and have its first effects in Britain's American colonies. There were several reasons for this: First, British victories against France in the Seven Years' War (1756–63) extended Britain's possessions in the Caribbean and allowed for an increase in the supply of sugar reaching the mother country, temporarily forcing down its price. But the decline was not permanent because the British returned captured French sugar islands after the war, and the commodity's price in the British market, protected by restrictive regulations, recovered. However, increasing absentee ownership, rising slave prices, soil exhaustion in older islands, natural disasters, and slave unrest caused a rise in production costs. The outbreak of the American Revolution in the 1770s, which cut off the major source of island supplies, aggravated the situation. Planters, however, did not curb but rather expanded production, spurred by an economic boom in the 1790s. Jamaican planters, particularly, extended cultivation. Nevertheless, the French island of Saint Domingue produced more sugar, more cheaply, and undercut the British sugar price in Europe. The British simply could not compete because of the high production costs associated with their sugar industry. Some people began to question the whole process of British sugar production, and the most glaringly expensive factor in this production was slavery.

But economic stress does not adequately explain the British antislavery movement. Indeed, the movement achieved its first successes during a period when the sugar industry had, however briefly, regained its profitability. Moreover, similar crises among the Spanish or Portuguese had not led to the same questioning of human bondage. One historian explains the distinctive British reaction as being the result of a different historical background than that of the Iberian nations. The Iberian peninsula (Spain and Portugal) had experienced slavery continuously from the time of the Roman Empire, and Iberians transported the institution to their colonies overseas as an ancient practice.

But slavery had died or was dying in northwestern Europe, and Englishmen readopted it in the 16th century mainly as a way to secure profits in tropical climes. They did not, however, approve of it at home. Where Iberians saw a familiar pattern of relationships because of their long slave tradition, Britons saw something new and relatively strange. Slavery was an institution for the colonies but not for Britain or the British. This does not mean that there were no slaves in Britain, for an estimated 14,000 resided there in the 18th century. But slaveholding was increasingly seen as an immoral choice, not part of British tradition.

One of the social, intellectual, and religious currents that forced people within the British Empire to look more closely at bonded labor was evangelical Protestantism. Millennialism (taken from the biblical prophecy in Revelations of Christ's 1,000-year reign on earth), which suggested the idea that man's sinful nature can be changed and that the world can be transformed into a heaven on earth, was an important feature of this outlook. It prompted much self-reflection. Millennialists equated slavery with sin and reform with virtue, and thus many of them became abolitionists. The ideas of the equality of all men before God and the necessity of free will for salvation were also sources of antislavery beliefs. Many Protestants considered free will to be essential to a conversion experience that emphasized personal commitment, and slavery permitted no free exercise of will.

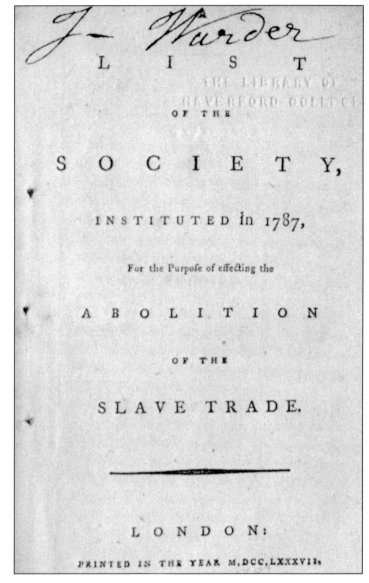

Antislavery groups sprang up throughout England during the latter part of the 18th century. They helped to bring about an end to the Atlantic slave trade.

Another intellectual concept was the Enlightenment. Beginning in the late 17th century, the European philosophical movement known as the Enlightenment developed around a number of concepts. The most important of these were a confidence in human reason as a guide to wisdom, a rejection of ignorance and superstition, a firm belief in the basic goodness of humankind, and a certainty that society, through reason, could be perfected. Eighteenth-century Enlightenment thought, particularly the idea of natural equality and the notion that society departed from that principle when it instituted slavery, also supported abolition. These philosophical ideas intersected with religious ones: From both perspectives, slavery was seen as wrong and society could and ought to be reformed.

But it took economic change, which placed increasing emphasis on free labor and free trade, and a move away from the restrictive trading system derived from mercantilism, to make the arguments of abolitionists most effective. Mercantilism was an economic philosophy based on the concept that a nation's wealth depended on its supply of precious metals or other commodities, such as gold and silver (bullion) or jewels. These could be obtained through trade or conquest. A nation's colonies existed to aid the mother country in achieving wealth by supplying these commodities directly or by producing items that could be traded for them. Ideally, a colony that did not yield bullion directly produced raw materials that could be rendered into products that would bring in bullion. Slavery was not a necessary component of mercantilism except that it came to be considered the most effective and efficient means of raising the tropical products that created the wealth of 18th-century European empires.

The Scottish philosopher Adam Smith cast doubt on this relationship. In his *Theory of Moral Sentiments* (1759) and *The Wealth of Nations* (1775), he argued that slavery was inefficient as well as brutal and, in fact, not the most profitable system. "The experience of all ages and nations," Smith claimed, "demonstrates that the work done by slaves, though it appears to cost only their maintenance, is in the end the dearest of all." It encouraged idleness, Smith argued, and retarded progress. Neither enforced labor nor restricted trade brought the greatest material or social reward.

In North America, even before the revolutionary era, the beliefs of some Protestant sects led them to consider the injustice of slavery. As early as 1688 a Quaker group in Germantown, Pennsylvania, spoke out against the institution, and in 1693 Quakers published the first anti-slavery tract in America. Quakers were not only concerned about their personal salvation but had a commitment to social reform as well. Their antislavery sentiments increased in the 18th century as individual meetings, or congregations, took a stand against holding slaves. They were joined in their stance by members of other sects as a result of the Great Awakening.

Having ousted the French from the continent, the British government developed reorganization schemes designed to govern the empire more effectively and economically. These efforts ended a practice that had left colonials largely to their own affairs. In practical terms, the new policies brought much greater interference by the British Parliament in the colonists' daily lives—an intrusion the colonists resented. Most disturbing was Parliament's claim of the power to tax, formerly assumed by provincial legislatures. Americans viewed these innovations as disruptive of harmony, running counter to an ancient and valuable relationship, and corrosive of traditional liberties. What began as a struggle for traditional English rights (such as the principle that they could not be taxed without their consent), however, was extended under the influence of Enlightenment philosophy into a struggle for liberty as a natural (rather than an English) right. This struggle forced white Americans to consider the plight of blacks.

The Massachusetts patriot James Otis made this connection most clearly in 1764 when, in response to the Sugar Act, he declared that "the Colonists are by the law of nature free born, as indeed all men are, white or black." Skin color, hair texture, or other physical characteristics were not a logical basis on which to base enslavement. Or, as another revolutionary put it, "That all black persons should be slaves is as ridiculous as that law of a certain country that all red-haired persons should be hanged." He referred to *The Spirit of Laws* (1748), a book by the French Enlightenment philosopher Baron de Montesquieu that made fun of prejudice by describing a country where that was the custom.

But blacks were not satisfied to let others make their case for them. They, too, were affected by revolutionary ideology and were quite prepared to use it to argue for their own freedom. This was particularly the case for New England blacks, who, of all slaves, had the greatest opportunity to attain literacy. Thus in April 1773 four Massachusetts slaves

Four slaves requesting their freedom sent this letter to the Colonial Assembly of Massachusetts in 1773. The slaves compared their plight to that of the American patriots who were demanding their own freedom from England. Their request was denied.

BOSTON, APRIL 20th, 1773.

SIR,

THE efforts made by the legislative of this province in their last sessions to free themselves from slavery, gave us, who are in that deplorable state, a high degree of satisfaction. We expect great things from men who have made such a noble stand against the designs of their *fellow-men* to enslave them. We cannot but wish and hope Sir, that you will have the same grand object, we mean civil and religious liberty, in view in your next session. The divine spirit of *freedom*, seems to fire every humane breast on this continent, except such as are bribed to assist in executing the execrable plan.

WE are very sensible that it would be highly detrimental to our present masters, if we were allowed to demand all that of *right* belongs to us for past services ; this we disclaim. Even the *Spaniards*, who have not those sublime ideas of freedom that English men have, are conscious that they have no right to all the services of their fellow-men, we mean the *Africans*, whom they have purchased with their money ; therefore they allow them one day in a week to work for themselve, to enable them to earn money to purchase the residue of their time, which they have a right to demand in such portions as they are able to pay for (a due appraizment of their services being first made, which always stands at the purchase money.) We do not pretend to dictate to you Sir, or to the honorable Assembly, of which you are a member : We acknowledge our obligations to you for what you have already done, but as the people of this province seem to be actuated by the principles of equity and justice, we cannot but expect your house will again take our deplorable case into serious consideration, and give us that ample relief which, *as men*, we have a natural right to.

BUT since the wise and righteous governor of the universe, has permitted our fellow men to make us slaves, we bow in submission to him, and determine to behave in such a manner, as that we may have reason to expect the divine approbation of, and assistance in, our peaceable and lawful attempts to gain our freedom.

WE are willing to submit to such regulations and laws, as may be made relative to us, until we leave the province, which we determine to do as soon as we can from our joynt labours procure money to transport ourselves to some part of the coast of *Africa*, where we propose a settlement. We are very desirous that you should have instructions relative to us, from your town, therefore we pray you to communicate this letter to them, and ask this favor for us.

In behalf of our fellow slaves in this province,
And by order of their Committee.

PETER BESTES,
SAMBO FREEMAN,
FELIX HOLBROOK,
CHESTER JOIE.

For the REPRESENTATIVE of the town of *Thompson*

addressed a letter to the Colonial House of Representatives stating that "the efforts made by the legislature of the province in their last sessions to free themselves from slavery, gave us, who are in that deplorable state, a high degree of satisfaction." They went on to suggest that they, too, desired freedom.

They adopted a peculiar strategy in pressing their case: "We are very sensible that it would be highly detrimental to our present masters, if we were allowed to demand all that of *right* belongs to us." But, they continued, "Even the *Spaniards*, who have not those sublime ideas of freedom that Englishmen have, are conscious that they have no right to all the services of . . . the *Africans*, who they have purchased." So they simply asked to be allowed one day a week to work for themselves to accumulate the money to buy their freedom. The House tabled the petition. When the blacks appealed to Governor Thomas Hutchinson, he said that he could do nothing for them.

After the Declaration of Independence was signed, petitions to the Massachusetts legislature from blacks became a little more aggressive. In New Hampshire blacks argued that "the God of nature gave them life and freedom, upon the terms of the most perfect equality with other men" and that "private and public tyranny and slavery are alike detestable to minds conscious of the equal dignity of human nature."

At the same time, free blacks moved against other aspects of discrimination. Although they were subject to taxation, free blacks in Massachusetts and elsewhere could not vote or hold office. Consequently, in February 1780 a group of blacks, under the leadership of a prominent local businessman, Paul Cuffe, and his brother John, took further advantage of revolutionary philosophy. They suggested to the legislature that "while we are not allowed the privilege of freemen of the state, having no vote or influence in the election with those that tax us, yet many of our own color, as is well known, have cheerfully entered the field of battle in defence of the common cause, and that as we conceive against a similar exertion of power in regard to taxation." In other words, they desired to extend to themselves the principle of no taxation without representation. Indeed, as part of the struggle, the Cuffes refused to pay taxes in 1778, 1779, and 1780. As a result, in December 1780 they were jailed. Three months later they admitted defeat and paid their back taxes, but they renewed their complaint.

Because blacks refused to let the argument die, it was difficult for New Englanders and other colonials to escape the logic of the revolution. Moreover, as the Cuffes noted, blacks were among the first to shed their blood in the common cause. Phillis Wheatley had a good chance to view the event of March 5, 1770, that went down in history as the Boston Massacre, for it took place just down the street from the Wheatley mansion at King Street and Mackerel Lane, where she still lived.

In 1770, British soldiers fired on an unruly Boston mob, killing five people, including Crispus Attucks, a former slave who had run away from his master 20 years earlier. This engraving by Boston patriot Paul Revere inaccurately shows the British soldiers ruthlessly firing on a peaceful crowd.

Boston citizens were outraged by the presence of British troops sent to quell unrest in their city, caused by their protests of British policies, and they taunted them whenever they could. On this particular evening, a crowd gathered around a sentinel stationed at the Custom House, who was accused of mistreating a young boy. They pelted him with snowballs and pieces of ice and forced him to cry for help. When a small squad of redcoats came to his aid, the town fire bell pealed the need for reinforcement of the citizenry and, a newspaper reported, "numerous bodies immediately assembled in the streets."

Among those answering the summons was a tall young mulatto, stout and strong, who left the dinner table at a local tavern to head a group of 20 to 30 men, armed with sticks and clubs, who approached the scene of the disturbance. The mulatto's name was Crispus Attucks, and 20 years earlier he had run away from the man who claimed to own him in Framingham, Massachusetts. Who provoked the musket fire that followed is not entirely clear, but the volley wounded eight men and killed five. Attucks, imposing in stature and at the front of the crowd, was perhaps the first to die. He certainly became the focus of attention during the ensuing controversy.

The radical patriot Samuel Adams, accepting the report of an eyewitness, sought to exonerate the citizens and blame the soldiers for the debacle by reporting that Attucks "was leaning upon a stick when he fell, which certainly was not a threatening posture." But another eyewitness, the slave of a Boston official, testified that "a stout man with a long cord wood stick, threw himself in, and made a blow at the officer." He then attacked a soldier and "held the bayonet with his left hand, and twitched it and cried, kill the dogs, knock them over." This witness identified the attacker as Crispus Attucks. Attucks became a revolutionary hero, celebrated as "the first to defy, and the first to die" in the cause of colonial liberty.

Other blacks fought more personal battles. In April 1781, 28-year-old Quok Walker left his master's service. He did so without permission and was sheltered by a neighbor, who employed him. His master discovered Walker, assaulted him with a whip handle, and charged the neighbor with enticing away his property. For his part, Walker brought suit against his master for assault and battery. The case came down to the issue of whether slavery was legally defensible, justifying the use of force. The master's lawyer argued that custom and usage of the country made slavery legal. Walker's lawyer argued,

The 29th Regiment have already left us, and the 14th Regiment are following them, so that we expect the Town will soon be clear of all the Troops. The Wisdom and true Policy of his Majesty's Council and Col. Dalrymple the Commander appear in this Measure. Two Regiments in the midst of this populous City ; and the Inhabitants justly incensed : Those of the neighbouring Towns actually under Arms upon the first Report of the Massacre, and the Signal only wanting to bring in a few Hours to the Gates of this City many Thousands of our brave Brethren in the Country, deeply affected with our Distresses, and to whom we are greatly obliged on this Occasion—No one knows where this would have ended, and what important Consequences even to the whole British Empire might have followed, which our Moderation & Loyalty upon so trying an Occasion, and our Faith in the Commander's Assurances have happily prevented.

Last Thursday, agreeable to a general Request of the Inhabitants, and by the Consent of Parents and Friends, were carried to their *Graves* in Succession, the Bodies of *Samuel Gray, Samuel Maverick, James Caldwell,* and *Crispus Attucks,* the unhappy Victims who fell in the bloody Massacre of the Monday Evening preceeding !

On this Occasion most of the Shops in Town were shut, all the Bells were ordered to toll a solemn Peal, as were also those in the neighboring Towns of Charlestown Roxbury, &c. The Procession began to move between the Hours of 4 and 5 in the Afternoon ; two of the unfortunate Sufferers, viz. Mess. *James Caldwell* and *Crispus Attucks,* who were Strangers, borne from Faneuil-Hall, attended by a numerous Train of Persons of all Ranks ; and the other two, viz. Mr. *Samuel Gray,* from the House of Mr. Benjamin Gray, (his Brother) on the North-side the Exchange, and Mr. *Maverick,* from the House of his distressed Mother Mrs. *Mary Maverick,* in Union-Street, each followed by their respective Relations and Friends : The several Hearses forming a Junction in King-Street, the Theatre of that inhuman Tragedy ! proceeded from thence thro' the Main-Street, lengthened by an immense Concourse of People, so numerous as to be obliged to follow in Ranks of six, and brought up by a long Train of Carriages belonging to the principal Gentry of the Town. The Bodies were deposited in one Vault in the middle Burying-ground : The aggravated Circumstances of their Death, the Distress and Sorrow visible in every Countenance, together with the peculiar Solemnity with which the whole Funeral was conducted.

This account of the burial of the victims of the Boston Massacre appeared in the Boston Gazette and Country Journal. *The coffin on the far right bears the initials of Crispus Attucks, the former slave who became a hero of the revolutionary era for his role in the incident.*

however, that custom and usage were unsustainable when they went against reason. The case eventually went to the Massachusetts Supreme Court. In coming to its decision in 1783, the court declared that since the state constitution of 1780 declared in its preamble that all men were born free and equal, slavery in the state was illegal. At the same time, it gave blacks who were taxed the right to vote. New Hampshire followed Massachusetts's lead when it decided that its Bill of Rights of 1783 forbade slavery, at least for those born after its adoption. Vermont was more forthright and prohibited slavery in its constitution of 1777.

While the judicial process worked its way in Massachusetts, Pennsylvania faced the problem head-on and became the first state to adopt a manumission, or freedom, law. As the home of Quakers, antislavery sentiment there was strong; many German immigrants, such as the Amish and Mennonites, also opposed the institution.

Perhaps no single person was more important in this process than Anthony Benezet. Born in France but forced to flee because of religious persecution, he and his family eventually settled in Pennsylvania. Converting to the Quaker faith, he early became active in the antislavery cause. He published a number of pamphlets attacking slavery and the slave trade, dramatizing the evils of the trade and removing all doubts that it had any humanitarian features. Moreover, he studied the history of Africa to prove that Africans had cultures and civilizations comparable to those of other people in the world, and he argued that the chains of bondage alone were responsible for any failings they showed in America. He undertook to educate Philadelphia blacks, establishing integrated schools for that purpose. His writings had influence far beyond his locality. Thomas Clarkson, a leader in the British antislavery campaign, took his stance after reading Benezet's *A Short Account of that Part of Africa, Inhabited by the Negroes* (1762). John Wesley, founder of the Methodists, used Benezet's *Some Historical Account of Guinea* (1771) as the basis of sermons he preached in Britain against the slave trade. When Pennsylvania's manumission bill reached the Assembly, Benezet worked with the legislators to ensure passage.

As the first abolition law passed in America, Pennsylvania's 1780 statute was viewed as the perfect expression of American revolutionary philosophy. It provided for a gradual freeing of slaves over a period of years, yet it was not the most liberal such law to be passed. It merely

Quaker leader Anthony Benezet actively supported the antislavery cause and sought to educate blacks in Philadelphia. He established integrated schools and published pamphlets attacking slavery and the slave trade.

came in advance of the rest, and along with Massachusetts and Vermont, Pennsylvania was one of the few states to end slavery before Britain's formal recognition of American independence.

But while blacks made use of revolutionary rhetoric to advance their freedom, and gave their blood in the colonial cause, they could not help but be reminded, even as they fought, that they were different. Thus, when blacks joined a crowd of Boston whites in an attack upon British soldiers in 1769, a Boston newspaper commented, "To behold Britons scourged by Negro drummers was a new and very disagreeable spectacle." And when a black man aided British soldiers against a Boston crowd in 1770, a townsman shouted, "You black rascal, what have you to do with white people's quarrels?" To which the black man replied, "I suppose I may look on."

This consciousness of difference caused a group of slaves in the town of Thompson, Massachusetts, to end their request for freedom in 1773 with the statement: "We are willing to submit to such regulations and laws, as may be made relative to us, until we leave the province, which we determine to do as soon as we can, from our joynt labours procure money to transport ourselves to some part of the Coast of *Africa*, where we propose a settlement." Even before the end of the 18th century, then, there was the feeling among some blacks that a return to Africa was desirable. These emigrationists felt that because racial oppression in America was so great, black people could develop only if they returned to the land of their forefathers. They also thought that a return to Africa would help them to free their enslaved brethren in the New World by illustrating the competitiveness of tropical products grown with free labor. Finally, they believed that they could take with them to Africa the gifts of Christianity and civilization and serve as the means to uplift what common prejudice held to be a backward continent.

These ideas found resonance among the Christian evangelists of Phillis Wheatley's acquaintance. In 1773, one conceived a plan for educating two New England blacks, a free man named John Quamino and a slave, Bristol Yamma, and sending them to Africa as missionaries. The outbreak of the Revolutionary War doomed the project, yet not before Wheatley was asked to join the venture. She responded to the request with a statement that expressed the opinion of most American blacks, who, born and bred in the country, felt they had a right to consider it their own:

> Why do you hon'd Sir, wish those poor men so much trouble as to carry me [on] so long a voyage? Upon my arrival, how like a Barbarian shou'd I look to the Natives; I promise that my tongue shall be quiet for a strong reason indeed, being an utter stranger to the Language. . . . Now to be Serious, This undertaking appears too hazardous and [I am] not sufficiently Eligible to go—And leave my British & American friends.

Wheatley's British and American friends would soon be at war, but the warfare provided other opportunities for blacks to achieve their freedom.

CHAPTER 2

BATTLE CRY OF FREEDOM

◇ ◇ ◇

*The flag carried
into battle by the
Bucks of America,
an all-black company
from Massachusetts
during the American
Revolution.*

Eight months before the American Declaration of Independence was proclaimed in Philadelphia on July 4, 1776, a man named Lymus declared his own independence. He told his master in Charleston, South Carolina, as his master reported in the *South Carolina Gazette,* that he would "be free, that he w[ould] serve no Man, and that he w[ould] be conquered or governed by no Man."

In the year following the Declaration, two black men in Massachusetts advanced a different claim to liberty. They "ship'd on board the Armed Brigantine *Freedom,*" as their friends related the story, "to fight ag[ains]t the Enemies of America." They thereby justified a claim to *personal* freedom. As their white compatriots announced, they "were volentieers [sic] in the business & ought to be considered in the same light as any other Sailors & by no means liable to be sold meerly because they are black." Somewhat earlier, a group of slaves in Boston, Massachusetts, devised still a different course. They petitioned the governor to propose, so Abigail Adams informed her husband John, that "they would fight for him provided he would arm them, and engage to liberate them if he conquered." The governor was General Thomas Gage, British commander in chief in America, and these slaves were clearly willing to fight on the British side if that would guarantee their emancipation. These people exemplify the claim of one noted African-American historian that black people in the revolution were more concerned about a principle than any one place or people—that principle being the natural right of human beings to their own person.

Later Americans, not to mention people at that time, would sometimes argue that African Americans were in no sense part of the community that fomented rebellion against Great Britain, or that issued the Declaration of Independence. This was the argument advanced by Chief Justice of the United States Roger Taney, for example, when he ruled in the Dred Scott decision of 1857 that blacks were not citizens of the United States.

Yet African Americans were motivated by the same desire for "life, liberty, and the pursuit of happiness" that animated other Americans. They were equally conscious of the natural rights philosophy of the Enlightenment and of the meaning of the phrases that Thomas Jefferson addressed to King George III. Thus black New Hampshire petitioners proclaimed: "Freedom is an inherent right of the human Species, not to be surrendered, but by Consent, for the sake of social Life." Abigail Adams expressed the same sentiments somewhat differently to her husband John. "I wish most sincerely," she wrote, "there was not a slave in the province; it always appeared a most iniquitous scheme to me to fight ourselves for what we are daily robbing and plundering from those who have as good a right to freedom as we have."

When the fighting broke out, therefore, African Americans were among the first to rally to patriot banners. As they fought to free their country, they also fought to free themselves. Thus the slave of New Hampshire general John Sullivan, told by his master that they were going to join the patriot army to fight for liberty, responded "that it would be a great satisfaction to know that he was indeed going to fight for *his* liberty." Sullivan, impressed by the justice of his cause, freed him on the spot. Peter Salem, of Framingham, Massachusetts, the place Crispus Attucks had fled to go to Boston, was freed by his owners so that he could enlist. He fought in the battles of Lexington and Concord in April 1775 and helped to fire the "shot heard round the world" that heralded the beginning of America's military struggle. In June he fought at the Battle of Bunker Hill, where the colonials were forced to retreat after inflicting heavy losses on the British. Salem is credited with killing a British officer who led the final assault, and his musket is preserved at the Bunker Hill Monument.

Salem Poor, a free black, also fought at Bunker Hill. He came to the attention of 14 officers who petitioned Congress to reward him for

Salem Poor, a free black who fought at Bunker Hill, so impressed 14 of the officers there that they sent this petition to Congress, asking that he be rewarded for his valor.

his bravery: "We declare that A Negro Man Called Salem Poor . . . behaved like an Experienced officer, as well as an Excellent Soldier." Although there is no record that Congress ever acknowledged him, he remained with the Continental army.

New England blacks were well situated to offer their services, for, despite laws prohibiting the practice, they had a history of duty in local militias. There simply were not enough white men willing or able to fill the ranks. African Americans served in 25 percent of Connecticut's militia companies and in noticeable numbers in other New England colonies. In spite of its relatively small black population, therefore, New England contributed more blacks to the Continental army than any other region. Rhode Island offered an all-black regiment, reported to be one of the few American regiments that enlisted for the entire war. A German officer in western Massachusetts in 1777 commented that "you never see a regiment in which there are not negroes, and there are well-built, strong, husky fellows among them." In the same year, another officer remarked on the presence of blacks among Massachusetts troops, but voiced an objection. Though he was pleased that they were able-bodied, he was not happy to see them mixed with whites. Patriot general Philip Schuyler, on a military campaign in upstate New York, expressed a more general objection to the presence of blacks. "Is it consistent with the Sons of Liberty," he asked, "to trust their all to be defended by slaves?"

Indeed, that was a question the colonials had to face as soon as the contending parties came to blows. In a country where slavery remained an important economic and social institution, few whites wanted the army to become a haven for runaway slaves. After the Continental army was formed in June 1775, commanding general Horatio Gates ordered that recruiters should not enlist "any stroller, negro, or vagabond," nor any deserter from the British army. He did not distinguish between slaves and free blacks. In September, the Continental Congress rejected a proposal of Edward Rutledge of South Carolina that blacks be totally excluded, but a council of generals in Cambridge, Massachusetts, adopted just such a policy the following month.

They took this position apparently in deference to George Washington, newly arrived commander in chief of the Continental army. Having scarcely ever been outside the confines of slaveholding Virginia and Maryland, he was appalled to find large numbers of blacks among the troops besieging the British in Boston in 1775. New England generals

The following LETTER *and* VERSES, *were written by the famous* Phillis Wheatley, *the African Poetess, and presented to his Excellency Gen.* Washington.

SIR,

I Have taken the freedom to addrefs your Excellency in the enclofed poem, and entreat your acceptance, though I am not infenfible of its inaccuracies. Your being appointed by the Grand Continental Congrefs to be Generaliffimo of the armies of North America, together with the fame of your virtues, excite fenfations not eafy to fupprefs. Your generofity, therefore, I prefume, will pardon the attempt. Wifhing your Excellency all poffible fuccefs in the great caufe you are fo generoufly engaged in. I am,

Your Excellency's moft obedient humble fervant,

Providence, *Oct.* 26, 1775.   PHILLIS WHEATLEY,

His Excellency Gen. Wafhington.

CEleftial choir! enthron'd in realms of light,
Columbia's fcenes of glorious toils I write.
While freedom's caufe her anxious breaft alarms,
She flafhes dreadful in refulgent arms.
See mother earth her offspring's fate bemoan,
And nations gaze at fcenes before unknown!
See the bright beams of heaven's revolving light
Involved in forrows and the veil of night!
  The goddefs comes, fhe moves divinely fair,
Olive and laurel binds her golden hair:
Wherever fhines this native of the fkies,
Unnumber'd charms and recent graces rife.
  Mufe! bow propitious while my pen relates
How pour her armies through a thoufand gates;
As when Eolus heaven's fair face deforms,
Enwrapp'd in tempeft and a night of ftorms;
Aftonifh'd ocean feels the wild uproar,
The refluent furges beat the founding fhore;
Or thick as leaves in Autumn's golden reign,
Such, and fo many, moves the warrior's train.
In bright array they feek the work of war,
Where high unfurl'd the enfign waves in air.
Shall I to Wafhington their praife recite?
Enough thou know'ft them in the fields of fight.
Thee, firft in place and honours,—we demand
The grace and glory of thy martial band.
Fam'd for thy valour, for thy virtues more,
Hear every tongue thy guardian aid implore!
  One century fcarce perform'd its deftin'd round,
When Gallic powers Columbia's fury found;
And fo may you, whoever dares difgrace
The land of freedom's heaven-defended race!
Fix'd are the eyes of nations on the fcales,
For in their hopes Columbia's arm prevails.
Anon Britannia droops the penfive head,
While round increafe the rifing hills of dead.
Ah! cruel blindnefs to Columbia's ftate!
Lament thy thirft of boundlefs power too late.
  Proceed, great chief, with virtue on thy fide,
Thy ev'ry action let the goddefs guide.
A crown, a manfion, and a throne that fhine,
With gold unfading, WASHINGTON! be thine.

After being appointed commander in chief of the Continental army, George Washington received this letter and poem from Phillis Wheatley.

insisted that they made good soldiers, but Washington persuaded them that the use of African-American troops would hinder cooperation with southern colonies. Washington, however, did not have the same emotional dislike of blacks that affected Thomas Jefferson. When he wrote a friend justifying the need to resist British tyranny, for example, Washington noted that if they failed to do so, "custom and use shall make us as tame and object slaves as the blacks we rule over with such arbitrary sway." In saying so, he related the status of blacks to their enslaved condition rather than to nature, suggested that anyone in the same circumstances would act the same way, and implied reservations about the practice of slavery itself. Moreover, his appraisal of Phillis Wheatley was distinctly different from that of Jefferson.

The celebrated poet wrote and sent the commander an elegy upon his accession to command. Washington responded that although he was not worthy of the homage, "the style and manner exhibit a striking proof of your poetic talents; in honor of which, and as a tribute justly due to you, I would have published the poem, had I not been apprehensive, that, while I only meant to give the world this new instance of your genius, I might have incurred the imputation of vanity." He invited her to visit him at headquarters if she were ever in the area. Both from inclination and considerations of policy, therefore, Washington was convinced to listen when free blacks expressed their dissatisfaction at exclusion. He authorized their reenlistment and put the matter before Congress. Congress backed the decision but forbade any new black enlistments. That policy, however, was to change.

Among the considerations influencing Washington was the action of the royal governor of Virginia. As the largest slaveholding colony, Virginia had reason to fear the effects of revolutionary thought on the slaves. Virginians had concrete reasons for their apprehensions, too, for some slaves took actions to gain their freedom by siding with the British. In November 1774, a small number secretly chose someone "who was to conduct them when the English troops should arrive—which," Virginia planter James Madison reported, "they foolishly thought would be very soon and that by revolting to them they should be rewarded with their freedom." Unfortunately for the conspirators, their plot was discovered and they were punished. Other plans were hatched, although, as Madison cautioned, "it is prudent such things should be concealed as well as suppressed," and we do not always know much about them. As the dispute between colonists and the mother country continued, bondsmen openly offered their services to the crown. The royal governor, John Murray, Lord Dunmore, refused an offer made to him in April 1775 and ordered the slaves "to go about their business." Indeed, a correspondent to the *Virginia Gazette* advised, he "threatened them with his severest resentment, should they presume to renew their application." At the same time, however, he made clear to the colonists that in the future he might reconsider and free and arm the slaves. Moreover, he expressed his confidence to Lord Dartmouth in London that, given sufficient sup-

Discharge papers given to Caesar Fideler on May 14, 1780. Fideler served with the Fifth Connecticut Regiment for three years. He was one of 5,000 blacks who fought for the Continental army against the British.

plies, he would have no trouble collecting "from among the *Indians*, negroes and other persons" a force capable of dealing with rebellious Virginians. Instead, he was forced to flee the capital, took refuge on a British warship, and contented himself with raiding colonial farms and plantations.

After defeating the colonists in a small engagement in November 1775, he decided to accept the blacks' offer of aid. He issued a proclamation on November 14, offering freedom to slaves and indentured servants of rebels who joined his troops. It was a decisive step, and he knew there could be no turning back. Yet the edict plainly was not a universal declaration of freedom. It applied only to the slaves of rebellious subjects and only to those able to join and fight. It nevertheless offered a clear choice that many accepted. One planter complained that his bondman's "elopement was from no cause of complaint . . . but from a determined resolution to get liberty, as he conceived, by flying to lord Dunmore."

But neither Lord Dunmore's proclamation nor the Declaration of Independence caused any immediate change in the colonials' determination to keep slaves out of the war. States from New England to Georgia forbade blacks to enlist. Manpower shortages alone caused these prohibitions to be overlooked. Free blacks often took the place of whites when states drafted soldiers, and recruiting officers, sometimes paid by the head, were not particular about the inductees' color. When, beginning in 1777, Congress ordered the states to meet quotas to fill patriot ranks, the process of black recruitment picked up speed. African Americans were commonly enlisted in New England after 1777 and Rhode Island became the first state to authorize slave enlistment in 1778. Maryland took the same step in 1780, and New York in 1781. Virginia refused to follow Maryland's lead in enlisting slaves but did permit the service of free blacks. Nevertheless, some Virginia masters sent slaves to serve in their stead, promising freedom but frequently not making good on those promises after the war. In 1783, when it became aware of the situation, the state government freed those people.

Only the Lower South resisted the trend to enlist black soldiers. Greatly outnumbered by their slaves, planters who inhabited the coastal lowland regions of South Carolina and Georgia (often simply referred to as the low country) feared the consequences of permitting slaves to bear arms. They were more dependent than their neighbors on black labor and proved correspondingly less receptive to the logic of revolutionary reasoning. Yet even there it had effects.

No one better exemplified this fact than John Laurens, an aide to George Washington and son of South Carolina planter Henry Laurens, a former slave trader and president of the Continental Congress. Educated in Geneva, Switzerland, John had become influenced by antislavery sentiments. Early in the revolution he proposed recruiting slave soldiers in exchange for their freedom. He wrote his father in January 1778 asking that he be given his inheritance in able-bodied slaves, whom he would form into a battalion to be freed at the war's close. Henry asked Washington's opinion. John replied: "He is convinced that the numerous tribes of blacks in the southern part of the continent offer a resource to us which should not be neglected." The following year the Continental Congress gave its assent to the project and recommended the course to South Carolina and Georgia. But the Lower South would not be moved.

The issue of slave soldiers was controversial because it offered a threat to slavery itself. And the threat to slavery was important because it involved rights of property. The right to be secure in possession of their property was one of the things the colonists accused the British king of taking away from them when he taxed them without their consent. Thus when the Virginia legislature formally rejected the use of slaves as soldiers it was because, as one man reported, it was "considered unjust, sacrificing the property of a part of the community to the exoneration of the rest." Or, to put it another way, it was not fair to ask some people to give up their property in order to save the property of others.

The outbreak of fighting provided blacks some say in the matter. They had a choice of sides, and an estimated 5,000 ultimately stood in Continental ranks. But the conflicted nature of their response was illustrated at the Battle of Great Bridge, fought on December 9, 1775, and described as the "Lexington of the South." This battle compelled Lord Dunmore to leave the soil of Virginia and operate thereafter offshore from naval vessels. Almost half of the British force of 600 consisted of African Americans of Dunmore's "Ethiopian

A sketch of a black soldier by Baron Von Closen, a German nobleman who fought in the American army against the British.

Regiment," who went into battle wearing sashes emblazoned with the words "Liberty to Slaves."

On the other side, a black spy for the Virginians tricked Dunmore into attack, and a free black from Portsmouth, William Flora, distinguished himself in the engagement. Flora was "the last sentinel that came into the breast work," an officer remembered, and "he did not leave his post until he had fired several times. Billy had to cross a plank to get to the breast work, and had fairly passed over it when he was seen to turn back, and deliberately take up the plank after him, amidst a shower of musket balls." At least 30 of the blacks on the British side were captured.

Although Dunmore was forced away, the specter of his proclamation hung over the region, and periodic raids conducted by the British produced numerous slave defections. Thomas Jefferson had a reputation as a kind master, but when redcoats visited his estate in 1781, 30 of his slaves left with them. Robert "Councillor" Carter (so called because of his position on the governor's council from 1758 to 1772, where he had advisory and legislative functions), another kindly patriarch, was unusual in that he had accepted the Baptist faith and was united with his servants in a religious community. He made a special plea to his slaves to stay. But when royal troops arrived at one of his outlying farms, the lure of personal freedom proved too great. Jefferson estimated that about 25,000 Virginia slaves left their owners during the war, and many had to endure considerable danger and hardship to do so. Yet they were willing to pay the cost. As a correspondent to a Pennsylvania newspaper suggested, "the defection of the Negroes, [even] of the most indulgent masters . . . shewed what little dependence ought to be placed on persons deprived of their natural liberty."

Conflict between families and neighbors was more frequent in the Lower South than in the Chesapeake, and it created a violent atmosphere in which slaves had to tread lightly. British invasion provoked a bitter struggle between supporters and opponents of the crown. Indeed, several Georgia and South Carolina planters moved their families and slaves to more peaceful Virginia after the redcoats came at the end of the 1770s. As in Virginia, blacks were cautiously welcoming. A slave guide helped British forces in Georgia to outflank and defeat patriot forces in 1779, and when royal troops landed along the Carolina coast in 1780 they

> **C H A R L E S T O W N,** October 20.
>
> The following are some of the reasons that have been assigned, why the assault on Savannah did not succeed, viz.
>
> 1st. The enemy having a much more numerous garrison than had been represented; being said to consist of about 1700 effective regulars, and a great number of sailors, marines, militia, armed blacks, &c.
>
> 2d. Their having the advantage of the presence, skill and activity of so able and indefatigable an officer as the Hon. Col. Maitland; who, while our army were obliged to wait for the bringing up proper cannon and mortars from the fleet, (which took up many days, and was attended with inconceivable difficulties, on account of the distance of the shipping, and a series of tempestuous weather) was night and day incessantly engaged in adding to the strength and number of the works, upon which, it is said, he employed upwards of 2000 negroes.

In 1779, after American and French troops tried unsuccessfully to capture Savannah from the British, this newspaper account of the battle attributes the defeat to the British having "a great number of sailors, marines, militia, and armed blacks." As many as 20,000 African Americans served with the British during the American Revolution.

likewise had to depend on slave knowledge of the terrain. Many landowners abandoned their farms and plantations, leaving servants and white women and children to fend for themselves.

The British recruited blacks as guides or spies, as laborers to perform the heavy and exhausting work of building roads and fortifications, and some to serve as soldiers. Perhaps as many as 20,000 African Americans served with the British in one capacity or another, and 5,000 to 6,000 left with them when they evacuated Charleston in 1782. A large number of slaves—maybe most (like many whites)—took no side but pursued their well-being as best they could in a situation of military uncertainty and social upheaval. Some fled to Charleston or Savannah and tried to pass as free people. Some continued to run plantations, with or without a white man's presence, assuming greater independence in the process. These were, after all, their homes, and the only places—outside of one of the contending armies—where they had any chance to secure a livelihood. In a period of chronic shortages of food, clothing, and other supplies, their old homesteads were sometimes the safest place to be. Of course, no guarantee existed even there, for marauding forces of one side or the other regularly confiscated whatever they needed and frequently destroyed the rest.

The remaining alternative for blacks (as for whites) was to migrate to some region away from the fighting. Some did so, retreating into the wilderness to form independent communities of their own. Some formed or became members of roving bands, occasionally interracial, that added to the disorder. They roamed the countryside, taking what they could for their own benefit. Some joined patriot fighting units such as that of South Carolina's "Swamp Fox" Francis Marion, who bedeviled the British with lightning raids and then melted away into Carolina's forests, marshes, or swamps. No slave was safe roaming about, however; capture could mean being sold, punished, or executed. It took considerable courage, therefore, even to run to the invader. In view of all the upheaval, some blacks welcomed the return of landowners and peace.

But warfare weakened slavery and provided bondsmen with at least a few options. They were limited because neither Britons nor white Americans were prepared to allow open black rebellion. Neither Britons nor white Americans could envision or accept a black republic. The only practical choices were to seek as much freedom as possible within the framework of revolutionary ideology in America or to trust the word of the British when they promised an eventual emancipation, there or elsewhere. Those who stayed on plantations accepted the realities of their condition but extended the boundaries of their servitude considerably, often acting virtually as free men.

The Pennsylvania Gazette and Weekly Advertiser *printed this account of a black man named Ty, who was loyal to the British and led 20 men, both black and white, in an attack on American forces. Ty's group managed to take two prisoners and captured horses and ammunition.*

Extract of a letter from Monmouth county, June 12.
" Ty, with his party of about 20 blacks and whites, last Friday afternoon took and carried off prisoners, Capt. Barns Smock and Gilbert Vanmater; at the same time spiked up the iron four pounder at Capt. Smock's house, but took no ammunition: Two of the artillery horses, and two of Capt. Smock's horses, were likewise taken off."

The above-mentioned Ty is a Negroe, who bears the title of Colonel, and commands a motly crew at Sandy-Hook.

Despite the planters' nightmares, war and revolution provoked no slave insurrection. Throughout the colonies bound men and women rattled the chains of servitude and voiced their hopes of liberation. Abigail Adams complained about "a conspiracy of . . . negroes" in Boston who offered to fight for the British, and devoutly wished no one was enslaved there. A white woman in Philadelphia spoke sharply to a black man on the streets who did not give way before her and was told to "stay . . . 'till Lord Dunmore and his black regiment come, and then we will see who is to take the wall." Incidents such as these discomforted another Philadelphia gentlewoman who "dream'd of our Negroes and cou'd not get them out of My Mind . . . am Uneasy about them . . . had no rest." It was in the South, however, where most slaves resided, and the threat of violence loomed largest, that the effects were greatest.

Thomas Jefferson proclaimed in the Declaration of Independence that all men were created equal, but he had reservations about the capabilities of blacks.

About one-quarter of South Carolina slaves fled. There was even more movement in Georgia where, in response to British invasion, more than a third of the slave population walked away. No previous event in North American slavery equaled the slave exodus from Georgia, either in its size or consequences for undermining the institution. In the South as a whole, slave flight during the Revolution was of such an extent and character that it can almost be viewed as a kind of slave revolt.

While slaveholding colonials were zealous about guarding their claims to bondsmen they already possessed, they were less secure about arguing for the right to buy and sell them. They were particularly squeamish about the purchase of those newly brought from Africa. If the works of Anthony Benezet did anything, they dramatized the horrifying conditions under which the overseas slave trade was conducted. In those circumstances, the human rights of the captive were magnified and the property rights of the slave catcher or of the prospective buyer were greatly diminished.

Virginians had no difficulty, therefore, in attacking the slave trade. The Virginia constitution of 1776 accused the British king of an "inhuman use of his negative" in preventing the colony from excluding slaves, and Thomas Jefferson made the same charge in the Declaration of Independence. King George, Jefferson wrote, had "waged cruel war against human nature itself, violating its most sacred rights of life and liberty in the person of a distant people who never offended him, captivating and carrying them into slavery in another hemisphere, or to incur miserable death in their transportation thither." Never mind that the king had never forced any Virginian to buy slaves, nor that the prohibitive duties or taxes that Virginians and other colonists had placed on slaves before the Revolution (which is what Jefferson referred to) had been assessed for economic and social rather than humanitarian reasons. The fact is that the Atlantic slave trade was a horror difficult to ignore in a period of heightened humanitarian sensitivity.

For a combination of reasons, then, Americans moved against the slave trade. In New England, where slavery was relatively less important, legislatures began to terminate the trade with the first stirrings of revolutionary ardor. Rhode Island made the connection plain with a comment in its abolition law that "those who are desirous of enjoying all the advantages of liberty themselves, should be willing to extend personal liberty to others." When the Continental Congress decided in October 1774 to prohibit the import of slaves, however, it did so as part of a nonimportation agreement designed to bring economic pressure against British merchants rather than because the trade was morally objectionable. Colonials intended these merchants to put pressure on Parliament to change its policies. When Virginia, North Carolina, and Georgia prohibited the trade, it had more to do with economic considerations and political pressure against the British government than with humanity. Nevertheless, the Congress reaffirmed its prohibition in 1776 and no state reopened the trade thereafter, except those in the Lower South. By their activities, therefore, blacks forced their masters to see some of the contradictions in their fight against England and laid the groundwork for a new birth of freedom.

1775

By His Excellency the Right Honorable JOHN Earl of DUNMORE, His
Majesty's Lieutenant and Governor General of the Colony and Dominion of
Virginia, and Vice Admiral of the same.

A PROCLAMATION.

AS I have ever entertained Hopes, that an Accommodation might have
taken Place between GREAT-BRITAIN and this Colony, without being
compelled by my Duty to this most disagreeable but now absolutely necessary
Step, rendered so by a Body of armed Men unlawfully assembled, firing on His
MAJESTY's Tenders, and the formation of an Army, and that Army now on
their March to attack His Majesty's Troops and destroy the well disposed Subjects of this Colony. To defeat such treasonable Purposes, and that all such
Traitors, and their Abettors, may be brought to Justice, and that the Peace, and
good Order of this Colony may be again restored, which the ordinary Course
of the Civil Law is unable to effect; I have thought fit to issue this my Proclamation, hereby declaring, that until the aforesaid good Purposes can be obtained, I do in Virtue of the Power and Authority to ME given, by His Majesty, determine to execute Martial Law, and cause the same to be executed
throughout this Colony: and to the end that Peace and good Order may the
sooner be restored, I do require every Person capable of bearing Arms, to resort
to His Majesty's STANDARD, or be looked upon as Traitors to His
Majesty's Crown and Government, and thereby become liable to the Penalty
the Law inflicts upon such Offences; such as forfeiture of Life, confiscation of
Lands, &c. &c. And I do hereby further declare all indented Servants, Negroes,
or others, (appertaining to Rebels,) free that are able and willing to bear Arms,
they joining His Majesty's Troops as soon as may be, for the more speedily
reducing this Colony to a proper Sense of their Duty, to His Majesty's
Crown and Dignity. I do further order, and require, all His Majesty's Leige
Subjects, to retain their Quitrents, or any other Taxes due or that may become
due, in their own Custody, till such Time as Peace may be again restored to this
at present most unhappy Country, or demanded of them for their former salu-
tary Purposes, by Officers properly authorised to receive the same.

GIVEN under my Hand on board the Ship WILLIAM, off NORFOLK,
the 7th Day of NOVEMBER, in the SIXTEENTH Year of His Majesty's Reign.

DUNMORE.

(GOD save the KING.)

CHAPTER 3
BLACKS AND THE BRITISH
◇ ◇ ◇

The royal governor of Virginia, Lord Dunmore, issued this proclamation on November 7, 1775, granting freedom to any slave who managed to escape from his master and join the British forces.

As Americans wrestled with the question of what to do about the slaves, the British, unhampered by any inconvenient declaration of human equality, did likewise. Their West Indian empire as well as the southern portion of the North American colonies, which they still claimed, were based on slave labor. They had little interest in encouraging a social revolution that, if successful on the continent, might affect their holdings in the Caribbean. Moreover, they shrank from the prospect of being part of a bloody slave insurrection. Finally, they, too, generally accepted principles of white superiority that prevented them from considering a workable alliance with African Americans on terms approaching equality. It was clear, however, that blacks would have to be taken into account in a conflict in which they were an inevitable part.

An initial strategy was to use the black presence as a threat against the colonials. Thus General Gage warned South Carolinians that if they continued their opposition to Great Britain "it may happen that your Rice and Indigo will be brought to market by negroes instead of white people." This was not a pleasing prospect for either Britons or Americans, and proposals for emancipating southern slaves were not favorably received in Parliament. Lord Dunmore's proclamation and various other proposals to arm and free slaves caused public debate in England, for they were viewed as a shameful departure from a tradition opposed to using slaves against free people. Edmund Burke, a member of Parliament who supported the Americans, even considered such a policy

VIRGINIA, *Dec.* 14, 1775.

By the **REPRESENTATIVES** *of the* **PEOPLE** *of the Colony and Dominion of* **VIRGINIA,** *assembled in* **GENERAL CONVENTION.**

A DECLARATION.

WHEREAS lord Dunmore, by his proclamation, dated on board the ship William, off Norfolk, the 7th day of November 1775, hath offered freedom to such able-bodied slaves as are willing to join him, and take up arms, against the good people of this colony, giving thereby encouragement to a general insurrection, which may induce a necessity of inflicting the severest punishments upon those unhappy people, already deluded by his base and insidious arts; and whereas, by an act of the General Assembly now in force in this colony, it is enacted, that all negro or other slaves, conspiring to rebel or make insurrection, shall suffer death, and be excluded all benefit of clergy: We think it proper to declare, that all slaves who have been, or shall be seduced, by his lordship's proclamation, or other arts, to desert their masters' service, and take up arms against the inhabitants of this colony, shall be liable to such punishment as shall hereafter be directed by the General Convention. And to the end that all such, who have taken this unlawful and wicked step, may return in safety to their duty, and escape the punishment due to their crimes, we hereby promise pardon to them, they surrendering themselves to col. William Woodford, or any other commander of our troops, and not appearing in arms after the publication hereof. And we do farther earnestly recommend it to all humane and benevolent persons in this colony to explain and make known this our offer of mercy to those unfortunate people.

EDMUND PENDLETON, president.

hypocritical. Why, he wondered, should blacks accept "an offer of freedom from that very nation which has sold them to their present masters?" Doubts about the slaves' level of "civilization," an unwillingness to take the slaves of loyalists, and a fear of driving Americans to extremes beyond hope of reconciliation, all argued against a slave alliance. In both Virginia and North Carolina, royal governors who sought to use slaves spurred colonials to rage and brought royal forces to defeat.

Unfortunately for the British and their American opponents, African Americans were not prepared to stand idly by while others decided their fate. If they were to be pawns in a game of chicken or chess, they would not be passive ones. They forced the hands of both Lord Dunmore and George Washington, and the use of blacks by one side reinforced the use of blacks by the other. But it was the shift of warfare to the South,

In response to Lord Dunmore's proclamation, Virginia's General Convention issued this statement threatening death to any slave caught trying to join the British side, while offering pardons to any slave who surrendered to the Continental army.

particularly the Lower South, where blacks frequently outnumbered whites in the general population, that sealed the British decision to utilize blacks, and changed their outlook toward the employment of black troops in other regions.

When Sir Henry Clinton, who replaced Gage as commander in chief of British forces in America, prepared to invade South Carolina in 1779, he began with the Philipsburg Proclamation. It was issued from his headquarters, Philipsburg Manor on the Hudson River in New York, on June 30. He declared that blacks taken in service with the patriots would be sold for the benefit of the crown, but that those who ran away to the British would be protected.

A policy provoked by military considerations rather than by humanitarian motives, it nevertheless chipped away at the foundations of slavery. It challenged blacks to take the British side. It did not formally offer them freedom but promised self-determination that was little short of it. Moreover, those who signed on as "pioneers," or laborers, to perform the drudgery of cleaning camp, building or repairing roads or bridges, constructing fortifications, or simply being on hand to take care of whatever undesirable tasks came up, were promised manumission in return for their devotion to duty. The same gift was held out to those who worked under British direction on agricultural estates or public works, or to the few enrolled as soldiers. African Americans took the bait in significant numbers.

Service with the British was not always to their liking, however. A policy prompted by military necessity was guided by military reasoning, and neither humanity nor fair play stood in the way of decisions that treated blacks harshly. They received fewer and inferior rations than white soldiers. They were not as well clothed. Their housing was inadequate and overcrowded. They were often overworked. They were consequently highly susceptible to disease, particularly various smallpox epidemics that afflicted the low country. Large numbers of them died. Nor were they exempt from sale for the use of the army when circumstances suggested that course.

Since the British army sought to maintain social order in regions it conquered, it had no philosophical objection to suppressing slave rebellions, particularly those directed against loyal subjects. It pledged to return the slaves of those whites who had remained loyal to the crown or to replace them with those of patriots. The degree to which slaves could

> To His Excellency Sir Henry Clinton Commander in Chief of His Majesty's Forces in North Amerie &c. &c. &c.
>
> We some of your Excellency's old Company of Black Pioneers, beg leave to Address your Excellency wishing you a happy new Year and the greatest Success in all your Public and Private undertakings and assure Your Excellency that we remain
>
> Your Excellency's
> most faithful and
> most humble Servants
>
> N York
> 1st Jany 1781
> The Black Pioneers

view the British army as an army of liberation, therefore, was very limited indeed. No wonder it did not evoke wholesale desertions from the colonials.

Nonetheless the pull of freedom was great and the chance of leaving bondage improved as the British moved toward defeat. Manpower shortages and a demonstrated black resistance to tropical diseases prompted General Alexander Leslie to recruit black troops seriously beginning in 1779. The successful use of blacks in South Carolina caught

Sir Henry Clinton, commander in chief of British forces in North America, received this New Year's greeting in 1781 from a company of black scouts.

the attention of other British officers and served as the precedent for the use of black soldiers in the West Indies. Shortly before the British left the Carolina coast, Jamaica's governor enrolled a battalion of troops from among the free black and colored, or mixed race, people of Charleston. They formed the Black Carolina Corps, which served in Jamaica and elsewhere, and they took with them American ideas about the rights of man. By the 1790s, Britain utilized black troops extensively to support its Caribbean empire.

When the British left the United States at the end of the war, the question of what to do about blacks who had sought their protection proved a source of controversy. Planters wanted their human property returned, but the new British commander in chief, Sir Guy Carleton, felt that the commitments made in previous proclamations of freedom to slaves who joined them ought to be honored.

The old slave dealer Henry Laurens, despite periodic expressions of sympathy for the Africans—and notwithstanding his son's championship of slave battalions—remained keenly aware of the property interests involved. He inserted a provision in the treaty ending the war, the Treaty of Paris of 1783, that obliged the British to return fugitive slaves. Sir Guy thought that would be dishonorable. He interpreted the clause to mean that he should shelter no more fugitives and gave orders to turn back any who had newly come in. Only those who had been with the army for a year or more would receive his protection. But those already with the army were, in his opinion, already free and no longer to be considered property. Or if they were, that issue would have to be solved by some kind of money transaction, for he was not prepared to violate the word of British officers by returning them. Nor could he believe that had been the intention of the government. British ministers, he said, could not possibly have agreed to such a "notorious breach of the public faith to-wards people of any complection." If the royal army's relationship with blacks had not always been the most admirable, at least at the end one general took the high ground and saved many blacks from a return to servitude.

George Washington stuck with the American position that the British ought to return fugitive slaves to their former owners. Yet compared to others who insisted firmly on the return of all slaves, Washington was unusually sensitive in this regard. He seemed resigned to the inevitable. "[S]everal of my own are with the Enemy," he reflected, "but I scarce ever bestowed a thought on them; they have so many doors through which they can escape from New York, that scarce any thing but an inclination to return . . . will restore many." He thereby indicated a property awareness strongly modified by a revolutionary spirit that was rapidly diminishing in the wake of American victory. If Thomas Jefferson most clearly expressed the ideals of the revolution, Washington, of all the slaveholding leaders of the revolution, came closest to practicing these ideals insofar as blacks are concerned. He certainly desired the return of property, but he was prepared to accept a black man's rejection of that status. In contrast to Jefferson, he provided in his will for the freeing of many of his slaves.

Boston King exemplifies the reasons many slaves left for the British side and also why many others did not. He was born in South Carolina, and as a child he performed many of the ordinary tasks common to plantation life, such as running errands and minding cattle. After an apprenticeship to a carpenter, he became a skilled laborer. He also had an uncommon experience. At one point he worked around racehorses, which permitted him a degree of travel. The job occasioned some hardship because the head groom was unkind and once made him go without shoes through the winter because he happened to lose a boot. His mentor in carpentry was also mean and mistreated him until his owner, Richard Waring, threatened to withdraw him from service.

Although King had an easygoing master, his experiences with other white folk made him wary of slaveholders' kindness and conditioned him to be receptive to British offers of freedom. He accompanied his master outside of Charleston—or Charles Town as it was then known—during the redcoats' occupation. But, he wrote in his memoirs,

Sir Henry Clinton led the British forces in North America from 1778 to 1782. He, along with other British officers, often benefited from the skill and knowledge of runaway slaves but would not shelter those who belonged to Americans loyal to England.

> having obtained leave one day to see my parents, who lived about 12 miles off, and it being late before I could go, I was obliged to borrow [a horse]; but a servant of my master's took the horse to go a little journey, and stayed two or three days longer than he ought. This involved me in the greatest perplexity, and I expected the severest punishment, because the gentleman to whom the horse belonged was a very bad man, and knew not how to show

mercy. To escape his cruelty I determined to go to Charles-Town, and throw myself into the hand of the English . . . altho' I was most grieved at first, to be obliged to leave my friends, and remain among strangers."

Boston King eventually followed the British to New York City and there married Violet, a fugitive from North Carolina. Recaptured by the Americans, he was treated well but "sorely distressed at the thought of being again reduced to slavery, and separated from my wife and family." He managed to escape and return to his English protectors. Unlike white Americans, Boston King was not filled with joy at the end of the war, "for a report prevailed at New-York that all the slaves, in number 2,000, were to be delivered up to their masters, altho some of them had been three or four years among the English. This dreadful rumour filled us with inexpressible anguish and terror, especially when we saw our old masters coming from Virginia, North-Carolina, and other parts, and seizing upon their slaves in the streets of New-York, or even dragging them out of their beds. Many of the slaves had very cruel masters, so that the thoughts of returning home with them embittered life to us." King and other slaves were therefore highly appreciative of the position taken by British general Sir Guy Carleton. King and his wife received certificates of freedom and left with other loyalists for Nova Scotia.

Large numbers of blacks accompanied British forces when they departed the coastal cities of Savannah, Charleston, Philadelphia, Boston, and New York at various times during the war and especially during the final evacuations. Besides Nova Scotia and the West Indies, London was also a destination for several hundred North American blacks. In London, which had a significant black population in the 18th century, these new arrivals attracted the attention of antislavery activists and fueled a concern about the treatment of blacks in England and the British Empire. The Somerset case of 1772 had established that English law did not recognize slavery in the kingdom itself, but it had not applied to the colonies.

Blacks on the streets of London, however, could not be ignored, particularly since so many were destitute and reduced to begging. For unlike white loyalists, who were frequently compensated for their losses and supported until they were reestablished in Britain and elsewhere, African Americans were given little assistance. The British government assumed that since they had nothing to begin with, former slaves should be thankful merely for their freedom.

In the absence of governmental concern, a group of humanitarian businessmen formed the Black Poor Committee in 1786 to provide temporary relief. They also persuaded the Lords of the Treasury to grant aid to the most needy, although, as it turned out, this was not enough for bare subsistence. At this point Henry Smeathman, an amateur botanist who had spent some time on the coast of Africa, offered to rid the committee and the government of their unwanted charges by settling them in Sierra Leone, on the west coast of Africa. Abolitionist Granville Sharp became involved with the scheme and even drew up a plan of government. In spite of Sharp's involvement, the initial idea seems to have been to get blacks out of England over all other considerations. The humanitarian and religious reasons usually associated with the settlement of Sierra Leone were not much in evidence when the colony was first proposed.

William Wilberforce was one of the leaders of the antislavery movement in England who backed the creation of the colony of Sierra Leone, in West Africa. The colony became a haven for former slaves.

Nevertheless, once the scheme was advanced, it become the focus of antislavery groups as a possible means of attacking the slave system by introducing free labor into Africa. Quakers had begun petitioning Parliament against the slave trade and formed the majority of the Society for Abolition of the Slave Trade, founded in 1787, in which they were allied with other evangelicals. Their activities made the slave trade a public issue by 1787, at the time the Sierra Leone expedition was getting underway.

Despite Sharp's continued activity, the men around whom the movement focused were Thomas Clarkson and William Wilberforce. Clarkson's interest resulted from his decision in 1785 to enter a contest sponsored by Cambridge University. It offered a prize for the best essay on the question, "Is it lawful to make slaves of others against their will?" As he knew nothing about slavery or the slave trade, he read, among other things, Anthony Benezet's *Short Account of Africa* and set to work. He won the prize and a short time later received what he considered to be a divine mission to devote his life to abolition. He joined with Granville Sharp and others in the Society for the Abolition of the Slave Trade.

The role of Clarkson was primarily as researcher and writer. He was not a very good speaker, had little sense of humor, was somewhat petulant, and showed little inclination to compromise. Still, he had an immense capacity for work. He visited Liverpool, Bristol, and other slaving ports to gather data for use against the trade. He began a collection of horror instruments, such as thumbscrews, handcuffs, leg shackles, and mouth openers (which were used to force-feed slaves who sought to starve themselves to death) to illustrate the cruelty of the trade. He realized his limitations, though, and knew that, lacking oratorical skills, he was unlikely to become a captivating national leader. Someone would have to be found who had a gift for public speaking, preferably someone wealthy and well connected whom the slaving interests could not buy or intimidate. Such a man was William Wilberforce.

Born in Hull, England, Wilberforce was the son of a wealthy merchant. He was physically frail but brilliant and charming. His grandfather bequeathed him a fortune and he grew up addicted to the good life. He frequented the best clubs, kept company with prominent people, and took to gambling and heavy drinking. However, he was also an eloquent speaker as well as an amiable companion, and when he tired of dissipation he decided to enter Parliament. But Parliament bored him, too. He took a tour of Europe with a religious friend who converted him to evangelical Christianity and gave his life more meaning. He intended to resign from Parliament and find more useful employment until his friend Prime Minister William Pitt suggested that he involve himself in the abolitionist cause. A few parliamentary speeches brought him to the attention of the Society for the Abolition of the Slave Trade and he agreed to become its spokesman. He and Clarkson became close friends.

The two were dedicated to a common goal and complemented each other because each had qualities the other lacked. Together they mapped out a strategy. They decided to concentrate on the misfortunes suffered by English sailors engaged in the trade rather than on the Africans they enslaved, because they felt the English public would more likely be moved by the former. They also agreed to limit their attack to the trade and not malign slavery itself so as avoid alarming West Indian planters. They assured planters that their slave property would be more valuable and insurrections less likely if the trade were abolished.

The first of these conclusions they derived from the fairly obvious relationship between supply and demand: If the supply ceased and the demand remained constant, the value of bondsmen already on, or capable to be put on, the market would rise. The second conclusion was put forward because newly imported Africans were frequently thought to be responsible for slave rebellions. But Wilberforce and Clarkson also felt that they could undermine the argument for slavery if a free labor colony in Africa, raising competing tropical products, proved successful. Such a colony would benefit English industrialists by furnishing raw materials for English manufacturers and providing a market for English goods. Moreover, such a colony would be only the starting point for opening a much larger African market, one that would absorb much more of Britain's production than its West Indian colonies. An African market would provide more work for English workingmen and more wealth for the wealthy. In other words, the abolitionists hoped to convince the English public and English business interests that they had more to gain than to lose by ending the slave trade and, ultimately, slavery.

A total of 459 people left Portsmouth, England, for the African coast on February 23, 1787, to found the colony of Sierra Leone. Most were black, but almost a quarter were white, most of them white women married to black men. At least half of the emigrants were former slaves from North America. Olaudah Equiano, of the Ibo ethnic group in western Africa, had been kidnapped from his African homeland and enslaved in the Americas. But he had regained his freedom, immigrated to England, and been appointed by the navy commissioners as commissary for the voyage. He was responsible for the settlers' supplies. He complained, however, that preparations were inadequate. Moreover, he charged the white man who supervised the venture with incompetence, dishonesty, and racism. The supervisor misappropriated funds for his own use, Equiano said, and treated blacks "the same as they do in the West Indies." Although Equiano's charges had merit, he was recalled, and white men were left in control.

The voyage, therefore, did not have an auspicious beginning and the settlement came close to failure. The settlers came at the wrong time of year for building and brought the wrong kind of seeds for planting. They quickly succumbed to disease. By September almost half the original colonists were dead and only a supply ship sent by Granville Sharp the following year saved the remainder.

Abolitionists now began to take a serious interest in the African enterprise, for it was clear that its failure would harm their cause. Among

THE
INTERESTING NARRATIVE
OF
THE LIFE
OF
OLAUDAH EQUIANO,
OR
GUSTAVUS VASSA,
THE AFRICAN.
WRITTEN BY HIMSELF.

VOL I.

Behold, God is my salvation : I will trust and not be afraid, for the Lord Jehovah is my strength and my song ; he also is become my salvation. And in that day shall ye say, Praise the Lord, call upon his name, declare his doings among the people, Isaiah xii. 2, 4.

FIRST AMERICAN EDITION.

NEW-YORK:
Printed and Sold by W. DURELL, at his Book-Store and Printing-Office, No. 19, Q. Street. M,DCC,XCI.

Olaudah Equiano was taken from his African home as a child and sold into slavery in the Americas. The extraordinary details of his life, described in his autobiography, captivated readers in England and in America.

other things, it would support the proslavery argument that blacks could not rule themselves and would work only under the threat of force; it would also ruin the vision of a free-labor society in Africa as a market for British manufactured goods. Thomas Clarkson, Granville Sharp, and William Wilberforce, therefore, were appointed as three of the directors of a new enterprise, the Sierra Leone Company.

What gave the colony a new lease on life was the arrival of immigrants from Nova Scotia, Canada. African-American migrants to that region had found harsh winters, rocky and infertile land, starvation, discrimination, and political limitations. Hardship faced both white and black refugees, but the blacks came with less of everything needed for their survival and were given less upon their arrival. In the meantime, Boston King recalled: "Many of the poor people were compelled to sell their best gowns for five pounds of flour, in order to support life. When they had parted with all their clothes, even to their blankets, several of them fell down dead in the streets through hunger. Some killed and eat [sic] their dogs and cats; and poverty and distress prevailed on every side."

John Clarkson, brother of Thomas, accompanied Thomas Peters, who had been a leader of the Black Pioneers, a British military unit formed in 1776, back to Canada, and in January 1792 they left Nova Scotia with almost 1,200 passengers for the Province of Freedom, as Sierra Leone was called. One of these was Henry Washington, who had run away from the American commander-in-chief in 1776. He proved to be a successful farmer in Sierra Leone until he was banished for involvement in a dispute over issues of taxation and representation in the African colony. His quarrel offers clear evidence that the settlers had not forgotten their American revolutionary experience.

Already the fight against slavery and the slave trade was beginning to have some impact. Britain was now the leading slave-trading nation, with the French not far behind. Prime Minister William Pitt attempted to negotiate an agreement with the French in 1787 for mutual abolition of the slave trade, but that attempt failed. Among other reasons, the French were not anxious to hamper the prosperity of their thriving sugar colony in Saint Domingue, in the Caribbean, which was heavily dependent on slaves.

The British Parliament nevertheless passed a law in 1788 to limit the number of slaves its own vessels could carry relative to their size. This law was designed to make the slave trade somewhat more humane by providing the captives more room and comfort. In 1789 Wilberforce introduced a motion in Parliament to abolish the British trade and began a series of hearings into the issue. Meanwhile, Clarkson set off for the continent to make contact with the Society of the Friends of the Blacks in France, formed in 1788 for the same purpose. He, like Pitt, hoped to coordinate the abolitionist activities of the two nations so that their opponents could not use a failure in one nation as an excuse for failure in the other. The outbreak of the French Revolution in 1789 and the subsequent slave rebellion in Saint Domingue made the slave trade's abolition impossible in the 1790s. Nevertheless a start had been made and African Americans had had something to do with it.

The influence of African Americans on this worldwide movement to end slavery operated at various levels. The American Revolutionary War provided African Americans a chance to fight for their freedom by playing one force against another. No other group more clearly saw the contradiction between revolutionary ideals and American practice. Occasionally, they succeeded in convincing their white compatriots to live up to their stated ideals of the natural equality of all people, or at least to recognize their inconsistency when they did not. Of course, the war also provided blacks an alternative course to liberty. Those who left the country took revolutionary notions with them—to Africa, to the West Indies, and elsewhere.

The war also cut off West Indian planters from supporters in North America and left them to fight the rising tide of abolitionism within the British Empire unaided. This was true not solely in political terms but in economic and social terms as well. They lost easy access to American supplies and to the American market for their molasses. They therefore became more dependent on the mother country and more vulnerable to imperial pressure. African-American immigrants into Britain forced the issue of slavery and caused people there to take a stand. They therefore helped to breathe new life into British abolitionism, contributing to the British attack on the slave trade and eventually on slavery itself. In their American homeland, however, the revolution had only limited success.

An ACT

For the Gradual Abolition of Slavery.

—

Sec. 1. BE *it enacted by the Council and General Assembly of this State, and it is hereby enacted by the authority of the same,* That every child born of a slave within this state, after the fourth day of July next, shall be free ; but shall remain the servant of the owner of his or her mother, and the executors, administrators or assigns of such owner, in the same manner as if such child had been bound to service by the trustees or overseers of the poor, and shall continue in such service, if a male, until the age of twenty-five years, and if a female until the age of twenty-one years.

2. *And be it enacted,* That every person being an inhabitant of this state, who shall be entitled to the service of a child born as aforesaid, after the said fourth day of July next, shall within nine months after the birth of such child, cause to be delivered to the clerk of the county whereof such person shall be an inhabitant, a certificate in writing, containing the name and addition of such person, and the name, age, and sex of the child so born ; which certificate, whether the same be delivered before or after the said nine months, shall be by the said clerk recorded in a book to be by him provided for that purpose ; and such record thereof shall be good evidence of the age of such child ; and the clerk of such county shall receive from said person twelve cents for every child so registered : and if any person shall neglect to deliver such certificate to the said clerk within said nine months, such person shall forfeit and pay for every such offence, five dollars, and the further sum of one dollar for every month such person shall neglect to deliver the same, to be sued for and recovered by any person who will sue for the same, the one half to the use of such prosecutor, and the residue to the use of the poor of the township in which such delinquent shall reside.

3. *And be it enacted,* That the person entitled to the service of any child born as aforesaid, may, nevertheless within one year after the birth of such child, elect to abandon such right ; in which case a notification of such abandonment, under the hand of such person, shall be filed with the clerk of the township, or where there may be a county poor-house established, then with the clerk of the board of trustees of said poor-house of the county in which such person shall reside ; but every child so abandoned shall be maintained by such person until such child arrives to the age of one year, and thereafter shall be considered as a pauper of such township or county, and liable to be bound out by the trustees or overseers of the poor in the same manner as other poor children are directed to be bound out, until, if a male, the age of twenty-five, and if a female, the age of twenty-one ; and such child, while such pauper, until it shall be bound out, shall be maintained by the trustees or overseers of the poor of such county or township, as the case may be, at the expence of this state; and for that purpose the director of the board of chosen freeholders of the county is hereby required, from time to time, to draw his warrant on the treasurer in favor of such trustees or overseers for the amount of such expence, not exceeding the rate of three dollars per month ; provided the accounts for the same be first certified and approved by such board of trustees, or the town committee of such township ; and every person who shall omit to notify such abandonment as aforesaid, shall be considered as having elected to retain the service of such child, and be liable for its maintenance until the period to which its servitude is limited as aforesaid.

A. Passed at Trenton, Feb. 15, 1804.

CHAPTER 4
SLAVERY AND FREEDOM IN THE NEW NATION

◇ ◇ ◇

Revolution and war in America, based on principles of natural rights and human equality, created an environment destructive to slavery. Yet there were definite limits to the effectiveness of these forces. Among the revolutionary generation there was no clear line drawn between human rights and property rights; no feeling that the one ought to come before the other.

Thus Pennsylvania's chief justice, denying a slave woman's claim to emancipation in 1815, wrote that "I know that freedom is to be favoured, but we have no right to favour it at the expense of property." Significantly, this case came from one of the nation's most liberal states. The judge's statement accurately captures the spirit of the earlier age. Rather than being banned by the state on the grounds of immorality, slavery was seen as something that had to be abolished voluntarily, usually with some form of compensation to the former slaveowners. This was not a direct compensation from the government. Most people thought that would be too great a public expense. Indeed, some radicals felt that, in a moral sense, if such a payment were to be made it ought to go to the bondsman in return for his unrequited toil rather than to his master.

Instead, the gradual emancipation laws enacted in most northern states provided for freedom for children of existing adult slaves born after a certain date, but not to those slaves themselves. In addition, the children were bound to serve their parents' master until sometime in

Most Northern states enacted laws like this one passed in New Jersey in 1804 that called for the gradual elimination of slavery. Starting in July 1804, according to the New Jersey law, any child born to a slave "shall remain the servant of the owner of his or her mother . . . until the age of twenty-five years [if male], and if a female until the age of twenty-one years."

their 20s, depending on the state. Slave owners thus continued to benefit from slave labor for some years after these acts were passed. Nevertheless, in the northern states, where the institution was not economically crucial nor its abolition regarded as too socially disruptive, slavery gradually ended.

By 1784 the new nation was already well along the way toward a division between a northern region of free states and a southern one of slave states. Yet that vision is most clear in hindsight. A person who lived at the time may not have considered that result a foregone conclusion. For one thing, slavery was still fairly strongly entrenched in New York and New Jersey. Proposals to end the institution there in 1785 and 1786, respectively, failed. Indeed, slavery expanded rapidly in New York during the 1790s, particularly in New York City. The surrounding rural population, which was largely Dutch, remained strongly wedded to bound labor.

In Virginia, by contrast, there was widespread antislavery sentiment and the legislature passed a law in 1782 making it easy for individuals to follow their conscience and free their slaves. Moreover, Delaware and Maryland, like New York and New Jersey, also debated ending slavery, in roughly the same period and with the same results; the measures failed. But unlike New York and New Jersey, they followed Virginia's example and made manumission easier than it had been, Delaware in 1787 and Maryland in 1790.

North Carolina had some difficulty making up its mind and adopted various pieces of contradictory legislation, but in all these states the free black population expanded considerably. North Carolina Quakers were particularly active in conveying the enslaved to freedom. They took advantage of every legal opportunity that was offered, including ensuring that slaves promised freedom in return for fighting were not reenslaved. They also bought bondsmen and let them pay off the debt and live as free people in all but name.

Yet there were distinct differences between the situation in New York and New Jersey and in the states south of Pennsylvania. African Americans were never more than about 10 percent of the population of these Middle Atlantic states. They made up almost a third of Virginia and Maryland and nearly as large a proportion in Delaware and North Carolina. Moreover, they were an important economic asset in the South. This was true equally in terms of their labor on farms and plantations, where they were a much higher percentage of the labor force than in the

A Roll of the proper Slaves of Thomas Jefferson. Jan. 14. 1774.

Monticello.

* Goliah.
* Hercules.
+ Jupiter. 1743.
* Gill.
* Fanny
+ Ned. 1760.
   Suckey 1765.
   Frankey. 1767.
   Gill. 1769.
* Quash
* Nell.
* Bella. 1757.
* Charles. 1760.
   Jenny. 1768.
* Betty
   Juno
* Toby junr. 1753.
— Luna. 1750.
* Cate. about 1747.
   Hannah 1770.
   Rachael. 1773.

Monticello.

+ George
+ Ursula.
   George.
   Bagwell.
   Archy.   1773
+ Frank   1757
+ Bett. 1759
+ Scilla. 1762.

* denotes a labourer in the ground.
+ denotes a titheable person following some o-
   ther occupation
— denotes a person discharged from labor on acct of age or infirmity

Thomas Jefferson kept this detailed list of the slaves who worked at his plantation. Despite his frequent expressions of a desire to free his slaves, he liberated only a few domestics.

North, and in their value as property. If they were freed, their labor could continue, of course, on a different basis. They could be paid instead of forced to work. But such a transformation still required a radical social and economic reorganization. Equally important, it required a mental restructuring.

Complicating the social issue was the question of race. Many white people did not think that white and black people could live together in peace—or, if they did so, only if one race was subordinate to the other. A prominent spokesman for this view was Thomas Jefferson. "Nothing is more certainly written in the book of fate than that these [black] people are to be free," he wrote on one occasion. "Nor is it less certain that the two races, equally free, cannot live in the same government."

He felt that peaceful relations would be prevented by prejudices that white people held against blacks and by the memories that black people had of the past injustices suffered from whites. Nor could he ever get over his feeling that black people were inferior to white people—that they did not have the same capabilities. Unlike some people, who felt that the environment of slavery was responsible for whatever shortcomings blacks exhibited, Jefferson struggled unsuccessfully against the suspicion that Africans were inferior by nature. This did not mean, however, that he intended to exclude African Americans from the inalienable rights he declared all men to have. His charge in the Declaration of

This section from Jefferson's handwritten draft of the Declaration of Independence contains a passage condemning the slave trade. This clause was omitted because of objections from Georgia and South Carolina planters who needed slaves and from New England shippers who sometimes engaged in slave trading.

Independence that King George III had "waged cruel war against human nature itself" in his pursuit of the slave trade, and that the king had thereby violated Africans' "most sacred rights of life and liberty," indicates that Jefferson regarded Africans and African Americans as full members of the human community. Moreover, to underline the point, he would later say that "whatever be their [the blacks'] degree of talent it is no measure of their rights. Because Sir Isaac Newton was superior to others in understanding, he was not therefore lord of the person or property of others." But his reasoning could not withstand his emotion, and his was a perspective widely shared in Virginia and elsewhere in the country. When Jefferson spoke of abolition, therefore, he also talked of removing blacks from the continent.

There were elements of this outlook in the Middle Atlantic states, but because the black population there was smaller, opposition to emancipation focused around the issues of property and compensation rather than on the social consequences of freeing blacks. Here the relationship between human rights and property rights could be more easily discussed. The problem surfaced everywhere, but it could be more easily separated from other issues in the North than in the South. Moreover, in New York and New Jersey, where slavery was generally more important than in New England, the discussion had more resonance. It affected more people more closely. Everywhere the issue arose it involved the well-being of people. Part of this equation included money and wealth and comfort. Another part included public and private safety and peace of mind. The various factors had to be weighed practically as well as philosophically.

"Private right and convenience," a correspondent to the New York *Argus* wrote during New York's debate about the ending of slavery, "always ought . . . [to] give way to public good." Because slavery was incompatible with the Declaration of Independence, *"Every negro in America is this moment of right, a freeman."* Furthermore, African Americans had earned their freedom, having shed their blood "on the field of battle bravely fighting for that liberty and independence we this day enjoy, and which we not only withhold from the present generation, but would, from nothing but sordid motives of gain rob from thousands of innocents, yet unborn."

A black man, William Hamilton, echoed these sentiments. He declared that he was "one of those whom the generality of men call Negroes[,] my fathers or ancestors [having come] from Africa[;] but I am a native of New York." He denied that "God appointed us" to be slaves of white people, and thought it scandalous that New Yorkers should pride themselves on their liberty when every part of the state "abounds with slavery and oppression."

Another writer moved directly to the confusion of human and property right. *"Property* in the persons and labors of other men, is a thing in itself absurd—it is a direct violation of the law of nature and society." Any proclamation to the contrary, therefore, ought to be void. When New York's manumission law was finally passed, a legislator, blaming opposition mainly on the Dutch, commented they "raved and swore . . . that we were robbing them of their property. We told them they had none, and could hold none in human flesh . . . and we passed the law."

Nevertheless, the freeing of slaves in New York and other Middle Atlantic states took a long time to happen. Fifteen years after the end of the Revolutionary War and 14 years after the final acts of liberation in New England, New York agreed to manumission. New Jersey did not do so until 20 years after the war. In the 1790s, while slavery was dead or dying in Philadelphia, it was still growing in New York City.

Slavery's usefulness and profitability in the 1780s and 1790s caused many to use it for their advantage. But also, in view of the undoubted antislavery sentiment of the time, many Northerners disassociated their institution from the horrors that were assumed to characterize slavery on Southern or Caribbean plantations. Slaves were "better off than the generality of the white poor," one New Jersey man argued, "who are obliged . . . to work harder than the slaves in general in this state." In this way slave owners could salve their consciences and at the same time attack slavery in the abstract. They could even work towards ending it locally, though they did so with no apparent urgency.

Several things countered this comfortable middle position among those inclined toward abolition in New York and meant that they would soon have to choose sides. One was the increasing numbers of free blacks, whose presence and activities weakened the institution. They served the slaves as examples of the possible. They were joined in their subversion by slaves themselves, who had a unique history in this region of being able to negotiate the conditions of their servitude. Black servitors had long been permitted to search for a new master if, for example, their current situation or location displeased them. A slaveholder's move from city to countryside might well prompt his servant to ask for permission to look for a new owner, so as to avoid exile to a rural location far from friends and family. Thus one white man offered his black woman for sale because of her "not chusing to go into the country where her masters family has lately removed." A slave named Jack approached a neighbor to offer *himself* for purchase. He said that "his mother and he could not agree," the prospective purchaser recorded in his diary, and "he had told his master he must have another house to live in." Many did not stop at trying to better their terms of servitude, however; in a revolutionary age, bondsmen sought also to arrange their freedom. Their increased desire for personal liberty marred any assumption that they were satisfied with bondage.

The immigration of refugees from the slave uprising in Saint Domingue was another factor disturbing the presumption of a benign servitude. White refugees frequently brought slaves with them and their severe treatment of them, conditioned by the harsher environment of the West Indies, strikingly illustrated the disadvantages of slave life wherever it existed. It was difficult to maintain the myth of a mild slavery when some were so obviously, and sometimes publicly, mistreated. For their part, Saint Dominguan slaves contributed significantly to slave unrest, further corroding the feeling of ease. Finally there were the activities of kidnappers who stole free blacks and sold them outside the state. They exhibited the crass economic nature of the institution, the unpleasant underbelly that was better left unexposed.

The New York Manumission Society arose as an answer to the problem of slavery in New York State. Formed in January 1785 in response to "violent attempts lately made to seize and export for sale several free Negroes," the society also aimed to promote eventual abolition. Its moral outrage was strictly limited, however. It did not engage in a scathing critique of slavery or slaveholders as they existed in New York, nor did it exclude slaveholders from membership. John Jay, the society's first president, owned slaves. He explained his apparent inconsistency: "I purchase slaves and manumit them when their faithful services shall have afforded a reasonable retribution." Whether his was an act of charity or hypocrisy, the fact that he and other slaveholders joined an anti-slavery society was indicative of the trend of the times. Even though they sometimes seemed to devote more effort to humanizing slavery than to getting rid of it, they nevertheless introduced gradual emancipation legislation and other measures to free and protect blacks. But if even some slaveholders could envision and work toward emancipation, one could reasonably foresee its doom. The ending of slavery in New York was drawn out and complicated. Its last manumission law, adopted in 1817, granted freedom to slaves born before July 4, 1799, to be effective July 4, 1827. But most slaves came to an agreement that provided their freedom considerably earlier than

Despite the fact that he was a slave owner, John Jay served as the first president of the New York Manumission Society. The group was formed in 1785 to promote the gradual abolition of slavery and to protect free blacks from being taken and sold into slavery.

that date. New Jersey moved more slowly, adopting comparable legislation in 1804 and 1846. It still had a few slaves at the time of the Civil War.

If abolition came slowly in the Middle Atlantic, it was indefinitely delayed farther south. The Upper South, the region north of South Carolina, was as much affected by the ideology of the Revolution as any area of the country. The commander of the Continental army, George Washington, the author of the Declaration of Independence, Thomas Jefferson, and many other prominent leaders of America's struggle against Great Britain were Virginians. Nearly all of them expressed reservations about slavery. Many, including Washington and Jefferson, expressed a desire to see it end.

Besides, there were more reasons than philosophy to support that position. Evangelical Methodists and Baptists, quite active in the

Chesapeake in the 1780s, carried out widespread religious revivals. They added Christian egalitarianism, or the belief that all men are equal in the sight of God, to the secular (or worldly) claims of equality advanced in the Revolution. Moreover, they were effective. Virginia's Robert Carter, one of the richest and most successful planters in the country, freed 500 slaves beginning in 1791, at least partly from religious conviction. "I have for some time past," he wrote in his deed of manumission, "been convinced that to retain them in Slavery is contrary to the true Principles of Religion and Justice, and that therefor[e] it was my Duty to manumit them."

Finally, there were economic considerations. Many planters in Virginia, Maryland, and Delaware began to shift from tobacco to cereal crops, such as wheat, oats, barley, and corn, beginning in the mid-18th century. They made this shift because of a fall in tobacco prices at the same time that the worldwide demand for food crops increased. They also moved to grains because tobacco so rapidly exhausts the soil. These new products did not require as much slave labor and many planters felt that they had a surplus of slaves. They were prepared to consider alternatives like the labor of free blacks. So for many reasons people in the Upper South could seriously consider manumission, and some moved from thought to action. Yet Southern revolutionaries ultimately contented themselves with making manumission a matter of personal conscience. Proposals for total abolition were considered but dismissed.

A major objection, as we have seen, had to do with race. One Southerner, still sensitive to the issue of bondage, tried in 1797 to put the best face on an obvious Revolutionary failure. "On inquiry," he explained, "it would not be found the fault of the southern states that slavery was tolerated, but their misfortune; but to liberate their slaves would be to act like madmen; it would be to injure all parts of the United States." He implied that Southerners were self-sacrificing statesmen for their willingness to keep black people in chains and under control, and he meant thereby to make slaveholding a patriotic duty. But by that time the economy had changed again. Slaveholders in the Upper South could now find a ready market for their slaves in the expanding cotton regions of the southwest. The momentum toward the abolition of slavery in the Upper South began to slip away.

The Lower South states of South Carolina and Georgia were largely exempt from the tenderness of conscience that afflicted the Upper

South. They had a plantation economy that was starved for bound black labor. While the loss of slaves during the war had inconvenienced Virginia planters, it had devastated those in the Lower South, whose prime concern was how soon the slave trade could resume. Moreover, slaves were a much higher percentage of their population; therefore the social and economic effects of the abolition of slavery were more significant. The relatively liberal period that flowered in the Upper South, therefore, had no counterpart in the Lower South. Some emancipations occurred, but these were prompted more by blood ties than abstract philosophy. Lower South planters were more likely to free their sons and daughters by slave mistresses than anyone else, so the free colored population that grew here was lighter-skinned than that in the Chesapeake, where manumissions were more often motivated by conscience.

Abolitionist pressure could in some instances be more effectively brought to bear at the national level, but the government formed under the Articles of Confederation (which were finally adopted in 1781) did not have much power. Having rejected a strong centralized government in Europe, few Americans were disposed to create a new one in their midst. The new states were jealous of their prerogatives and reluctant to surrender any more than necessary to what amounted to little more than a wartime alliance against England. Consequently, most activities that affected African Americans occurred at the state and local levels.

There was one crucial exception to this rule, and it had to do with territories to the west, where Americans expected their growing population would settle. Indeed, a struggle over the status of these lands kept the Articles from going into effect for years. Maryland, a small state, wanted the issue solved in such a way as to guarantee equal access to the West for the citizens of all the states, rather than trying to sort out conflicting and overlapping claims. Only when Maryland secured agreement that western territories would be considered the common property of all the states would it assent to the compact. Congress, under the Articles, therefore had to consider some plan for orderly settlement.

Thomas Jefferson offered a solution in his proposal for the Land Ordinance of 1784. Under his proposed law, slavery would have been prohibited in all western lands after 1800. This would have meant that all the territory west of the Alleghenies, north and south, would have prohibited slavery at the beginning of the 19th century. But the proposal would have allowed a 16-year period for slavery to become entrenched

The Articles of Confederation, the first constitution for the new nation, established a weak central government and allowed slavery in the existing states. However, slavery was forbidden in the Northwest Territory.

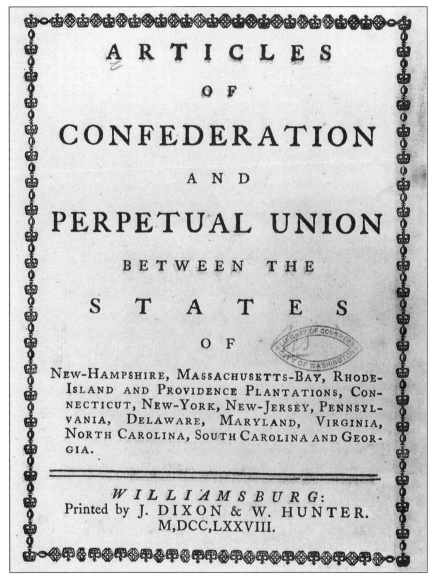

ARTICLES

OF

CONFEDERATION

AND

PERPETUAL UNION

BETWEEN THE

STATES

OF

NEW-HAMPSHIRE, MASSACHUSETTS-BAY, RHODE-ISLAND AND PROVIDENCE PLANTATIONS, CONNECTICUT, NEW-YORK, NEW-JERSEY, PENNSYLVANIA, DELAWARE, MARYLAND, VIRGINIA, NORTH CAROLINA, SOUTH CAROLINA AND GEORGIA.

WILLIAMSBURG:
Printed by J. DIXON & W. HUNTER.
M,DCC,LXXVIII.

before the law took effect. Some historians think that had that happened, the prohibition would have been repealed and slavery would have been allowed in all these western territories.

In any case, it failed by one vote. The measure that was adopted, the Northwest Ordinance of 1787, forbade slavery only in the area east of the Mississippi and north of the Ohio River, which was called the Northwest Territory. The ordinance did not free slaves already there, and it provided that any fugitive slaves who fled there should be returned to their masters. Slavery continued to exist in Indiana until 1818 and in Illinois until the 1840s. Nonetheless, an important principle had been established and slavery's spread had been curbed.

In making the Constitution of 1789, however, the Founders did not find revolutionary idealism all that useful. They had to reconcile many differences to form a strong nation, and to come to a compromise between the conflicting principles of freedom and property. In effect, this meant that blacks had to be compromised. This was not difficult for the framers of the Constitution because at the time of the Constitutional Convention in 1787 most states were slave states. Only in Pennsylvania and New England was slavery on the road to extinction. This did not mean that there could be no sectional division between North and South over this issue, because slavery was not nearly as important in northern places where it remained, nor did Northerners generally associate their practice with the southern one. Most Northerners expected its eventual end in their localities. In a real sense, slavery was already the South's "peculiar institution."

The process of compromise began as early as 1783, when Congress had to decide on a basis for raising national revenue. The states with the largest slave populations, Virginia and South Carolina, wanted land values to be the standard. Other states wanted to use population. Congress eventually settled on population but adopted a formula whereby a slave would count as three-fifths of a free person in the calculation. The measure never became part of the Articles of Confederation because it was not unanimously adopted by the individual states. Nonetheless, Congress had devised a workable formula and it was revived when delegates met at the Constitutional Convention in Philadelphia in 1787.

One of the first problems that had to be overcome at that convention involved representation in Congress. Edmund Randolph's Virginia Plan proposed altering the practice under the Articles whereby each state had one vote. Randolph proposed that a state's power in the national legislature be determined by its population. That proposal sparked sharp disagreement among the delegates, one usually described as along the lines of small states versus large ones. Yet the division was also between slave and free states, because obviously a state with a large slave population might turn into a small state if slaves were excluded. Southerners feared that in such a national union they would be consistently

Elbridge Gerry of Massachusetts was a delegate to the Constitutional Convention in Philadelphia in 1787. He was shocked at the notion put forth by Southern states that slaves should be included in measuring a state's population, thereby determining the number of representatives each state had in Congress.

outvoted by the larger free population of the North.

Many Northerners felt, however, that to count slaves equally with free people, or to count them at all, was ridiculous. Elbridge Gerry of Massachusetts, in protesting the three-fifths compromise eventually adopted (in which all slaves were counted as three-fifths of a free person to determine the number of representatives each state would be allowed in the House of Representatives), declared, "blacks are property, and are used to the southward as horses and cattle to the northward; and why should their representation be increased to the southward on account of the number of slaves, than horses or oxen to the north?" He did not argue the *morality* of keeping blacks as chattels in the same light as horses or oxen, nor did he dispute the assumption that there could be property in humankind. Yet such a criticism was implied, for no one would have suggested the representation of horses and oxen. Slave property was clearly of a different character than horses and oxen, at least in some respects. From the revolutionary perspective, that difference derived from the fact that they were human beings and as such deserved to be masters of their own destinies, but that attitude was of no use in an attempt to build a nation in association with those who insisted on the character of slaves as chattels. The revolutionaries had a choice: They could build two nations, based on opposing principles, or one nation, papering over contradictions and inconsistencies. They chose the latter course.

Northern delegates agreed to accept the principle that slaves would be counted for purposes of representation in Congress, and the South granted that they would not be counted as whole people. The sections settled upon the precedent-setting three-fifths compromise. Once that initial concession was made, other clauses respecting slave property could follow more easily. These included a fugitive slave provision, requiring runaway slaves to be returned to those who claimed them, and an agreement not to terminate the slave trade for 20 years. Northerners remained sensitive to the issue, however, and insisted that the word "slave" not appear in the Constitution. Slaves were instead referred to as "persons held to service or labor." Northerners even objected to placing the word "legal" before service, fearing that would suggest that black bondage was somehow legitimate, and disliked "servitude" as well as "slavery." Thus they could argue that they were being true to revolutionary principles at the same time that they denied them in practice.

The fact that the two sections were trying to reconcile opposites was no secret. This can be clearly seen in the way that Southerners defended, and felt that they had to defend, the new national compact in their arguments to convince their constituents to ratify it. Nor, in this instance, was there any difference between Upper and Lower South. "We have a security that the general government can never emancipate" the slaves, General Charles Cotesworth Pinckney of South Carolina argued, "for no such authority is granted; and it is admitted, on all hands, that the general government has no powers but what are expressly granted by the Constitution." He concluded, "In short, considering all circumstances, we have made the best terms for the security of this species of property it was in our power to make."

Moreover, the two foremost Virginians (George Washington and Thomas Jefferson), both of whom had expressed antislavery sentiments, decided that their political careers would be more secure if they ceased making public statements that might negatively affect their standing and influence. Consequently, when two British evangelists visited Washington in 1785 and asked him to sign a petition favoring emancipation, he refused. He said that it would not be appropriate. He indicated, however, that if the Virginia assembly agreed to consider the petition,

General Charles Cotesworth Pinckney of South Carolina helped to ensure that the Constitution of 1787 would protect slavery when he argued that his state and Georgia could not do without slaves. He also strongly supported the decision that slaves should be counted as people solely for the purpose of determining representation in the House of Representatives.

53,289 free males above 21 years of age.

17,763 free males between 16 and 21.

71,052 free males under 16.

142,104 free females of all ages.

———————

284,208 free inhabitants of all ages.

259,230 flaves of all ages.

———————

543,438 inhabitants, exclufive of the 8 counties from which were no returns. In thefe 8 counties in the years 1779 and 1780 were 3,161 militia. Say then,

3,161 free males above the age of 16.

3,161 ditto under 16.

6,322 free females.

———————

12,644 free inhabitants in thefe 8 counties. To find the number of flaves, fay, as 284,208 to 259,230, fo is 12,644 to 11,532. Adding the third of thefe numbers to the firft, and the fourth to the fecond, we have,

296,852 free inhabitants.

270,762 flaves.

———————

567,614 inhabitants of every age, fex, and condition. But 296,852, the number of free inhabitants, are to 270,762, the number of flaves, nearly as 11 to 10. Under the mild treatment our flaves experience, and their wholefome, though coarfe, food, this blot in our country increafes as faft, or fafter, than

L   the

This page from Jefferson's Notes on Virginia *shows that Virginia's slave population was just about equal to its white population.*

he would give his opinion of it. The assembly refused and Washington remained silent.

Jefferson took no more public actions on emancipation, or at least no more favorable ones, after he drafted the Land Ordinance of 1784. His official actions thereafter were all supportive of slavery. He resisted publication of his *Notes on Virginia* (originally written as private answers to questions from a French friend) because in it he had expressed mild antislavery sentiments. His fears appeared to be justified. A South Carolinian wrote to tell him of "the general alarm" that a particular "passage in your Notes occasioned amongst us. It is not easy to get rid of old prejudices, and the word 'emancipation' operates like an apparition upon a South Carolina planter."

There was every reason for politicians to be careful when it came to slavery, for there was widespread Southern support for it. Simultaneously, Southerners were equally attached to liberty. But if Northerners had followed the logic of revolutionary ideology to the conclusion that there could be no right of property in men, Southerners had rejected that deduction. "By Liberty in general," a Charleston minister declaimed, "I understand [not just civil liberty but] the Right every man has to pursue the natural, reasonable and religious dictates of his own mind; to enjoy the fruits of his own labour," and "to live upon one's own terms." It meant to be able to dispose absolutely of one's "property, as may best contribute to the support, ease, and advantage of himself and his family," and that would include property in slaves. He and other Southerners were quite willing, therefore, to deny Enlightenment principles and qualify revolutionary declarations. Consequently, when

Charles Cotesworth Pinckney recommended the Constitution to his constituents, despite its failure to include a bill of rights, he explained, "such bills generally begin with declaring that all men are by nature born free. Now, we should make that declaration with a very bad grace when a large part of our property consists in men who are actually born slaves."

Alternatively, Southerners defended themselves by disputing the assumption that blacks were fully men. It was true, as a South Carolinian wrote, that blacks had "human Forms," but, as another continued the argument, they were "beings of an inferior rank, and little exalted above brute creatures." They were thus fit objects as property. It followed that even as free people their defect of color, with all that it entailed, excluded them from citizenship. The revolution had been "a *family quarrel among equals*" in which "the Negroes had no concern."

Even in the North, where slavery was abolished, there was opposition to blacks as citizens equal to all others. This can be seen most clearly if one looks at the emancipation laws and controversies surrounding them. The Pennsylvania law (1780), the first to be passed, was also the most severe when compared to the emancipation acts of other Northern states passed between 1780 and 1804—this in a region dominated by Quakers and pretending to great liberality. No slave was immediately freed by it, and children born after March 1, 1780, had to serve until they were 28 years old before their freedom was recognized. This represented a tightening of an earlier draft of the law that freed females at 18 and males at 21.

In Massachusetts, where there were fewer blacks than in Pennsylvania, the uneasy feelings directed toward blacks were somewhat greater. The first state constitution, passed by the legislature in 1778 but rejected by the people, denied African Americans the right to vote; Pennsylvania's did not. The constitution of 1780 that Massachusetts finally adopted removed that prohibition, but blacks were strictly limited in their possibilities of employment and singled out in newspaper editorials for their supposed inability to work. Nor could they attend the schools that their taxes supported.

In 1788 Massachusetts prohibited all blacks except "citizens of the Emperor of Morocco" or those from another of the United States from residing within its territory for more than two months. The punishment for failure to obey the law was whipping. If the person still refused to leave the state, the punishment was supposed to be repeated every two months. It is unclear how seriously Massachusetts attempted to enforce the law, but several localities did take steps in that direction. In 1788, the city of Hanover, followed by Salem and Boston in 1800, asked the proscribed blacks to leave. On September 16, 1800, the Massachusetts *Mercury* published a list of all the blacks who came within the meaning of the statute, and they were to depart by October 10, 1800. It included people from 17 states, the West Indies, and several foreign countries. It does not appear that Massachusetts actually whipped anybody who defied the law, yet the statute had a chilling influence on black life. An early Connecticut law that was probably never enforced indicates the abiding New England attitude. Blacks could not buy land or establish a business in any town without that town's permission.

These and other prejudicial actions on the part of white citizens in Pennsylvania, Massachusetts, and elsewhere forced black people even more than whites to reflect on the relationship between freedom, revolutionary principles, slavery, and race. Even many of their supporters did not expect African Americans to prosper, and their enemies occasionally sought to stand in their way.

Yet bad as the situation was, this antipathy between black and white people was not as great as it would later become. Indeed, one student of Northern working-class people in New York found them to be refreshingly free of the racial stereotypes that common white folks were supposed to have. Although jokes about black people were common, they suggested a sympathy for and an identification with blacks. Both blacks and working-class whites were pictured as underdogs. Even so, there was enough of an edge to the jokes and sufficient force behind some of the actions to convince a small group of blacks that they should seek their fortune elsewhere.

One of the first black organizations to advance this aim was the Free African Union Society. Founded in 1780 in Newport, Rhode Island, it was a benevolent and moral improvement society as well as an agency of black emigration. It, like white abolitionists, was concerned with the plight of blacks. Thus it encouraged its members to refrain from idleness and drunkenness, tried to ensure that they made their marriages legal, and promoted investment in real estate. The society provided death benefits for the wives and children of deceased members and furnished loans for those in need. It also had a religious mission and held weekly services. Most importantly, the society tried to convoke a consensus that a return to Africa was the best course of action.

In January 1787, the Free African Union Society decided that it would establish its own settlement in Africa. About 70 people agreed to participate in the venture. Although many were African-born, they did not wish to merge with the indigenous people but rather to found a new country of their own. They wanted to get clear title to land somewhere on the continent in order to avoid conflicts with local people.

To this end, they sought out a rather flamboyant antislavery Quaker, William Thornton of Antigua, who was visiting the United States. A wealthy man, he was also a philanthropist who had developed a scheme to free his own slaves and set them up on a self-sustaining plantation in the West Indies. When island authorities discouraged that plan as a threat to slavery, he envisioned colonizing his blacks somewhere in Africa. Advised that free Christian African Americans also wanted to emigrate, Thornton revised his plans. He believed that the literate blacks in New England would perfectly complement agriculturally sophisticated West Indian blacks, who together could secure the colony's survival. One group would bring morality and industry and the other technical expertise. In Africa they would grow tropical products, repay the cost of their passage, and show slaveholders how the institution might be brought profitably to an end. They would establish a trade in products grown as free men, the value of which would rapidly surpass that of slave-grown crops.

Though the plan was laudable, the details were not. The Free African Union Society soon made it clear to Thornton that its members had no interest in becoming part of any venture in which they would be subservient to whites. They wanted to go someplace where they would be their own rulers. Nor were they willing to let Thornton act as their agent. They did feel, though, that if he was a truly charitable person, he might be willing to finance an advance group of Newport blacks to search for a suitable location. They also made contact with 75 blacks in Boston who had recently petitioned the Massachusetts legislature to provide assistance for their removal to Africa.

The petitioners there were led by Prince Hall, founder of the first African-American lodge of Freemasons. The Masons were a fraternal organization where men met to exchange news and ideas and occasionally to conduct religious services or discussions. They sought to overcome

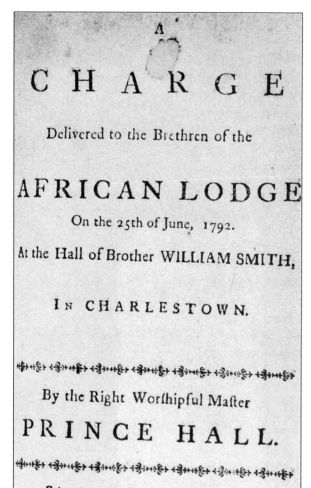

A

CHARGE

Delivered to the Brethren of the

AFRICAN LODGE

On the 25th of June, 1792.

At the Hall of Brother WILLIAM SMITH,

In CHARLESTOWN.

━━━━━━━━━━━━━━━━━━━━━

By the Right Worshipful Master

PRINCE HALL.

━━━━━━━━━━━━━━━━━━━━━

Printed at the Request of the Lodge.

Printed and Sold at the Bible and Heart, Cornhill, Boston.

The first African-American lodge of Freemasons was formed by Prince Hall in Boston in 1775.

social and religious divisions among men and to create greater understanding based on Enlightenment principles. Hall described the "true spirit of Masonry" as "love to God and universal love to all mankind." In 1775 he and 14 other blacks joined a lodge attached to a British regiment stationed in Boston. When the British left, they permitted the blacks to continue to meet as the African Lodge No. 1. Local Masons refused to recognize them, however, and they applied to England for a charter. Granted in 1784, the charter finally arrived in 1787. By that time, however, they were disillusioned—as individuals, if not as Masons—because, as they told Massachusetts's General Court, despite their freedom "we yet find ourselves, in many respects, in very disagreeable and disadvantageous circumstances; most of which must attend us, so long as we and our children live in America."

Having found kindred spirits in Boston, the Free African Union Society finally communicated with Granville Sharp in London, who was becoming involved with the settlement of Sierra Leone. But Sharp was not enthusiastic about American blacks coming over, especially if they insisted on acting independently. He made clear that if they came to Sierra Leone, they would have to act like English subjects and be bound by the common laws of England. The vision came to nought. Massachusetts was unwilling to put up any money to aid black emigration and Thornton, for all his planning, did not come through either. The blacks lacked the financial wherewithal to do it on their own.

Still, New England blacks would not give up. In 1789 the Free African Union Society addressed an appeal to compatriots in nearby

Providence, Rhode Island, proposing a new plan of emigration. In this document they advanced an early black nationalistic concept of uniting blacks in Africa, the West Indies, and the United States. Because they were "attended with many disadvantages and evils with respect to living" in the new American nation, they sought a nationhood of their own. They suggested a return to "the natives in Africa from whom we sprang, [they] being in heathenish darkness and sunk down in barbarity"— to whom African Americans would bring light. The success of the project would benefit Africans everywhere, for Africa's lack of civilization, as they saw it from a western point of view, was a source of shame. That lack was used to justify enslavement and the slave trade. If Africa were redeemed, the slave trade would cease, Africans overseas would be able to take pride in their homeland, the black man's humanity would be vindicated, and the link between blackness and slavery would be dissolved.

The Boston group invited the Providence blacks to join them in a united society that would meet every three months "to consider what can be done for our good, and for the good of all Affricans." "Now is the time," the Providence group would say in advancing yet another emigration plan in 1794, "if ever for us to try to Distinguish ourselves as the More remote we are situated from the white people the more we will be respected."

It is interesting to compare the plans developed by blacks (called "emigrationist") and those envisioned by whites (referred to as "colonizationist"). People like Jefferson who wanted blacks to depart were primarily concerned about the future and well-being of white people. Jefferson was not much interested in what happened to blacks, and his emancipation plans for Virginia would have compelled them to leave whether they wanted to or not.

People like Thornton, by contrast, had a religious and moral concern. They were interested in illustrating that blacks could progress in economic terms, both in America and Africa, because such advances would justify their struggles for black emancipation, validate their faith in the essential unity of humankind, and contribute to an end to black servitude worldwide. But they also doubted the ability of blacks and were sure that black people could make progress only under white direction. This attitude is called paternalism, that is, being like a parent who must oversee the activities of a child. African Americans, believing as much in their capability as their equality, thought they could and had to develop themselves largely on their own. They could welcome white help but objected to white domination. They were cultural hybrids and appreciated their American identity. Having adopted western values, they intended to westernize Africa, but they also wanted to cultivate a pride in being black. Only a great black nation would prove without doubt that blacks were not born to be slaves. But, because of lack of financing from white Americans and those African Americans who did have money, these early emigrationist movements all failed. For this reason, revolution in Haiti, which was developing even as these projects vanished, was an event of crucial significance.

Despite the movements to return to Africa, the period before the turn of the 19th century was one of hopefulness. In half the nation slavery had ended. This occurred not because it was unprofitable, or because there had been no opposition, or because the climate was uncongenial. It had happened largely as a result of war and revolution. And the revolution was not just political but social as well, a revolution in thinking as well as in acting that caused a part of the nation to confront prejudice and injustice and put them partially to rout. It was true that slavery had never been as important in the places where it ended as in those where it remained, that people who opposed it often had practical reasons as well as philosophical reasons for doing it, that many of those who favored freedom often had little confidence in the capacity of blacks to handle it. But a start had been made, and African Americans moved swiftly to take advantage of their opportunities.

CHAPTER 5
RICHARD ALLEN AND THE PROMISE OF FREEDOM

◇ ◇ ◇

O n April 12, 1787, Absalom Jones and Richard Allen "two men of the African race," as they described themselves in their Preamble and Articles of Association, "who, for their religious life and conversation have obtained a good report among men," met together with others in Philadelphia to form "some kind of religious society." Their Free African Society derived from "a love to the people of their complexion whom they beheld with sorrow, because of their irreligious and uncivilized state."

Jones and Allen's Free African Society was a mutual aid and moral improvement group that also had a religious bent. It was nonsectarian, in an attempt to attract African Americans of various Christian denominations, though it was closely associated with the Quakers. The society's rules specified that the clerk or treasurer should always be a Quaker, and eventually, meetings began with a period of silence in the Quaker fashion. The organization prohibited drunkenness among its members and provided death benefits.

Although it, like Newport's Free African Union Society, had been formed in the face of discrimination, and its assessment of the condition and immediate prospects of blacks in America was largely the same, its prescription was not. The Philadelphia group had none of the sense of mission or adventure evidenced in Newport. Or, rather, their sense of mission was distinctly different. They thought the solution to blacks' misfortune was self-improvement (with which New England blacks

Richard Allen was born a slave in Philadelphia in 1760 but went on to found the African Methodist Episcopal Church.

agreed), but otherwise they would depend on divine deliverance achieved through prayer and fasting. They rejected Newport's call for emigration. "This land," Richard Allen would later say about America, "which we have watered with our *tears* and *our blood* is now our *mother country*."

The different reactions of two African-American organizations who had basically the same diagnosis of the plight of black people in the United States is evidence of the "double consciousness" that the esteemed black scholar W. E. B. Du Bois wrote about at the turn of the 20th century. The African American, he suggested, "ever feels his twoness—an American, a Negro; two souls, two thoughts, two unreconciled strivings; two warring ideals in one dark body, whose dogged strength alone keeps it from being torn asunder." The people in these organizations memorialized their background by calling themselves African. They acknowledged their American identity by clinging to and seeking to spread various forms of Christianity. They adopted religious and cultural ideas of morality, hard work, thrift, and accumulation of wealth, and favored individual initiative together with group solidarity.

Within this common outlook, whether one stressed the African side of the equation and embraced black nationalism and a return to Africa, or seized upon America and more limited forms of separatism, depended to a great extent upon circumstances and personal inclination. In periods and locales where there seemed to be a chance for black progress in America, fewer were attracted to emigration; when and where the situation appeared less hopeful, more were inclined to leave. A firm religious belief and a conviction that, as Philadelphia responded to Newport, "the race is not to the swift, nor the battle to the strong," motivated some blacks to cling to their American identity, no matter what.

This attitude can be clearly seen in the lives of Richard Allen and Absalom Jones. Jones stayed in Philadelphia throughout the British occupation and remained with his master even after the English left. Allen also failed to run away, to either British or American forces. Both chose to take their chances under existing conditions and trust the promise of America. They had several reasons to do so.

Born a slave in Sussex County, Delaware, in 1747, Jones was at a young age removed from the fields and made a house boy. In that situation he was able to obtain some learning. From money earned around

Born into slavery in Delaware, Absalom Jones earned his freedom and became pastor of the African Episcopal Church of St. Thomas in Philadelphia in 1794.

the house, he "soon bought . . . a primer," he related in an autobiographical sketch, "and begged to be taught by any body that I found able and willing to give me the least instruction." When his master left Delaware for Pennsylvania in 1762, he sold Absalom's mother and brothers and sisters, having no need for a large slave family in Philadelphia. But he took the 15-year-old Absalom with him. Whatever distress the separation from family caused, the move nevertheless permitted Absalom to pursue an education. Philadelphia was the scene of much Quaker abolitionist sentiment, and people like Anthony Benezet had made some provision for black education. Despite having to work in his master's shop throughout the day, obliged "to store, pack up and carry out goods," a clerk taught him to write, and he secured his master's permission to attend school at night.

When he was 23, he married Mary, a neighbor's slave, and they determined to get their freedom. It made sense to secure Mary's first because that would allow their children to be born free, since children legally followed the condition of the mother. Absalom drew up a plea for his wife's freedom and carried it to prominent Quakers, some of whom lent, and others donated, the required cash. Working at night for wages, he and his wife repaid their loans. And while he beseeched his master to permit him to purchase himself, the couple saved enough money to buy a large house in a substantial neighborhood in January 1779, a few months after the British evacuated the city. Absalom owned property, therefore, while still a slave. Several more years passed before his master consented (in 1784) to his self-purchase. Bearing no animosity and receiving none in return, he continued to work in the store. When Richard Allen arrived in Philadelphia in 1786, Jones was a prominent black member of the largely white St. George's Methodist Church.

Richard Allen was born a slave in Philadelphia in 1760, but his master maintained a plantation in Delaware where Allen may have been raised. He was sold to a small slaveholder who worked a farm outside of Dover, Delaware, and his owner, a fair man, permitted him to join the local Methodist Society and attend classes after he was converted by itinerant preachers in the 1770s. His conversion may have been spurred by the sale of his parents and younger brothers and sisters shortly before his turn to religion. His conversion was no less sincere for that fact, and when neighbors criticized his master for permitting his slaves to attend frequent religious meetings, Allen and a remaining brother "held a council together . . . so that it should not be said that religion made us worse servants; we would work night and day to get our crops forward."

This diligence enabled Allen's owner to confound his critics, and, as Allen reported in his autobiography, he "often boasted of his slaves for their honesty and industry." Perhaps the example of his slaves as well as the teachings of itinerant Methodists moved him, too, to religion. But Methodism at this point was opposed to slavery, and a minister told him that his slaves would keep him out of heaven. In 1780, therefore, he encouraged Allen and his brother to purchase their freedom.

Allen then became a traveling preacher himself, taking the Methodist gospel as far afield as New York and South Carolina and into the backcountry. He supported himself by doing odd jobs and he preached to white and black audiences alike. In Radnor, Pennsylvania, 12 miles outside Philadelphia, where he had "walked until my feet became so sore and blistered . . . that I scarcely could bear them to the ground," he was forced to rest. Taken in and cared for by strangers, he repaid them by preaching. The townspeople took to him and persuaded him to tarry. "There were but few colored people in the neighborhood," he recalled; "most of my congregation was white. Some said, 'this man must be a man of God; I never heard such preaching before.'"

From there, in 1786, Allen received a call from St. George's to preach to the black congregants at 5:00 A.M. in order not to disturb white services. His ministry caught on. He soon had a group of blacks meeting separately for prayer meetings, among whom was Absalom Jones. Allen felt cramped within the confines of his relationship with St. George's, however, and proposed founding a separate black congregation. Other blacks agreed, but the white clergy was opposed. The minister, according to Allen, "used very insulting language to us to prevent us from going on," and tried to bar their meetings altogether. It was at this point that Allen and Jones organized the Free African Society as a nonsectarian organization. They conceived a plan to build an independent African-American community church that could attract black people without regard to denomination.

When the African Church of Philadelphia was formally proposed in 1791, its plan of church government was described as "so general as to embrace all, and yet so orthodox in cardinal points as to offend none." The group's justification for going its separate way was that a black church was more likely to attract black people than a white one. They reasoned that "men are more influenced by their moral equals than by their superiors . . . and . . . are more easily governed by persons chosen by themselves for that purpose, than by persons who are placed over them by accidental circumstances." In this phrase, directed at wealthy white people from whom they hoped to gain financial support, they combined democratic principles with strategic modesty and self-effacement. At the same time, they boldly declared their independence of paternalism (white supervision) and their rejection of discrimination within white denominations. White religious leaders, Methodist, Episcopalian, and Quaker, were virtually unanimous in opposition to the plan, revealing a clear unwillingness to relinquish their direction of black religious life. Moreover, they stood to lose their African-American congregants, who, whatever their humble status, sometimes made significant contributions to church affairs.

Not long after this effort was set in motion, an event occurred that is often said to have prompted the move toward black religious separation. Jones and Allen still worshipped at St. George's Methodist Church. Blacks, like other members, contributed to the church's expansion, but when the addition was completed, blacks were asked to retire to newly installed galleries. Even so, when Jones and Allen arrived for services one Sunday morning and knelt to pray above the seats where they formerly sat, they were approached by a trustee and asked to move. Jones requested him to wait until the prayer ended but the trustee said, "No, you must get up now, or I will call for aid and force you away." Jones again asked for a delay, but the trustee motioned for another to come to his aid. Just as the two were about to act the prayer ended and the blacks got up and walked out in a body. "They were," said Allen, "no more plagued with us in the church." This affair occurred in 1792, after plans for the African church were already in motion. Nevertheless, it reinforced the need for African Americans to form their own religious community.

Several years passed before the African church came into being. The disapproval of white religious leaders slowed donations, though such prominent people as George Washington, Thomas Jefferson, and Granville Sharp, in England, sent small contributions. Newport's Free African Union Society also made a donation. Blacks engaged in various efforts to raise money—but they were hindered in early 1793 by an influx of refugees from Saint Domingue and later in the year by a yellow fever epidemic. The latter furnished them an opportunity to show their public spirit by volunteering to nurse the ill and bury the dead, while many of the white people fled. The reception of Saint Domingue's white refugees, however, provided evidence of the black community's relative standing among the whites. Philadelphia's white citizens raised $12,000 in a few days for displaced slave owners, but the church for former slaves, costing less than a third as much, was delayed for several years for lack of money.

In July 1794 the African church opened its doors. Its members had decided to affiliate with the Episcopal church, feeling that some denominational connection was important for the security of the congregation. Only Jones and Allen voted for the Methodists. Calling itself the African Episcopal Church of St. Thomas, the congregation chose Absalom Jones as minister. The members sought to guarantee their local control by providing that only African Americans could be elected to church offices, except the minister and assistant minister, and that the congregation chose all church officers, including the minister and his assistant. They would permit themselves the possibility of choosing a white minister if they ever so desired, but they wanted the church to remain firmly in black hands. They would not surrender the revolutionary principle of self-government.

There were several reasons why blacks such as Jones and Allen were attracted to Methodism. As a new evangelical denomination, it had few ties with colonial slavery, and its founder, John Wesley, adopted an antislavery stance. Their religious egalitarianism reinforced revolutionary principles of equality, but, ironically, the fact that many Methodists were loyal to the British during the Revolution set them apart from patriotic groups, which were often proslavery. To many African Americans, Meth-

The Bethel African Methodist Episcopal Church in Philadelphia. After blacks refused to relinquish control of their new church building to the white-controlled national Methodist organization, they broke away and established an independent black Methodist church.

odists represented a strain of British antislavery in opposition to an increasingly proslavery American nation.

The itinerant nature of Methodist evangelicals increased their appeal to blacks (and poor white people), for they went out onto the roads and highways, into the fields and byways, to spread their message of salvation. They usually spoke in a direct, simple, emotional style and appealed to the heart rather than the intellect. Their methods had much in common with a traditional African religious outlook.

The emotional attraction is important because it is perhaps the one aspect of Methodism that made it more appealing than Quakerism, which shared many of Methodism's other attributes. Although Quakers held slaves, they were also among the earliest to express opposition to the practice and perhaps the first to act against it. They dominated early antislavery societies in Britain and America and were often loyal supporters of the English as well as pacifists during the years of revolutionary

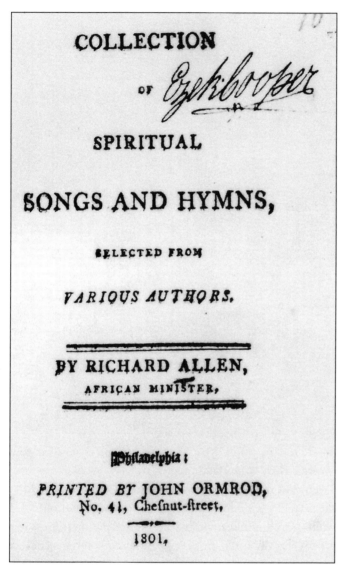

COLLECTION
OF *Ezekiboooper*

SPIRITUAL

SONGS AND HYMNS,

SELECTED FROM

VARIOUS AUTHORS.

BY RICHARD ALLEN,
AFRICAN MINISTER,

Philadelphia :

PRINTED BY JOHN ORMROD,
No. 41, Chefnut-ftreet,

1801,

In 1801, Richard Allen put together this hymnbook, the first compiled by an African American, for use by his congregation in Philadelphia. Although most of the hymns he selected were standards found in other hymnbooks, Allen also included several of his own compositions.

struggle. Their loyalism, however, seemed to discredit them more than it did the Methodists—perhaps because the Quakers were a more powerful group in colonial America—and it lessened the effectiveness of their antislavery efforts in the immediate postrevolutionary era. By contrast, the Methodists were less rigid about their abolitionst message and modified it in order to accommodate slaveholders in areas where slavery was legal. Despite their willingness to get along with slaveholders, the Methodists had an emotional appeal for blacks that the Quakers could not match.

Nevertheless, the African church affiliated with the Episcopalians. This probably had to do with what they perceived as Methodist shortcomings, for the Methodists, like other white people, often viewed blacks as childlike creatures who needed firm regulation. Blacks, they said, could not be trusted on their own. There was also at least occasional jealousy at the competition blacks offered. Thus one chronicler related that Richard Allen was encouraged to get off the circuit and remain in Philadelphia because a prominent white Methodist itinerant minister compared unfavorably.

By contrast, a black Methodist in New York, George White, was forced to preach outside the city for years because of the refusal of white Methodists in the urban area to accept him as an equal. These prejudicial attitudes encouraged black Methodists in New York City, led by James Varick, to leave the parent organization in 1796. They founded what later became the African Methodist Episcopal Zion church, with Varick as its first bishop. Similar experiences in Baltimore and other cities provoked similar actions. Not merely prejudice but blacks' own religious and social outlooks encouraged black separatism. For blacks, slavery was a sin and America could never be a truly Christian nation so long as it condoned slavery. They could not, as their fellow white Baptist and Methodist believers did, relegate it to politics nor consider it beyond the scope of religion.

Despite the problems, Allen remained committed to Methodism. He refused to accept leadership of the African church once it allied with Episcopalians, allowing the position to go to Jones instead. Allen persisted in building his own Methodist church. Established in the same year, a few blocks away from the black Episcopalians, it became the foundation of an independent black denomination, the African Methodist Episcopal church. "Mother Bethel" as Allen's Bethel African Methodist congregation was called, also attempted to safeguard its rights of local autonomy. It was a fight over that issue, and over ownership of the congregation's property, that prompted African Americans to leave the white-dominated Methodist organization and form their own denomination in 1816.

Once the black churches were established, they became the centers of black settlement in Philadelphia. The surrounding neighborhoods did not become black ghettos, because blacks were frequently interspersed with working-class whites and were not in the majority. But community activities among blacks were of necessity stronger than among their

white companions because they had few alternative sources of support. Nor could they move out of the neighborhood as easily.

Blacks also lived in other sections of the city and their numbers gave them a sense of possibilities. Philadelphia at the time had the largest free black population in the United States and developed the most thriving free black community. It had grown to 2,000 by 1790. At the same date, New York City, with as many blacks, was largely a slave city; indeed it possessed more bondspeople than any other American city except Charleston, South Carolina. Boston listed no slaves by that date but had a smaller black population. Because of its size and influence, Philadelphia is a good place to view the situation of blacks in the years immediately following the revolution. The stages of development there were paralleled in other Northern cities.

It was a relatively successful community, despite a postwar depression that affected large segments of the city. Newly freed blacks flocked to Philadelphia from rural Pennsylvania and neighboring areas of Delaware, Maryland, New Jersey, and even southern New England. They

This watercolor from the early 19th century offers a stereotypical view of blacks attending a church service in Philadelphia.

This early 19th-century watercolor of a black oysterman and clam seller illustrates one economic activity of free blacks in Philadelphia. African Americans virtually monopolized this enterprise.

sought gainful employment and economic independence. Men were drawn to seafaring, serving on merchant ships or working around the docks. By the beginning of the 19th century, about 20 percent of Philadelphia's merchant seamen were black. Women, who outnumbered men, reversing a disproportion in favor of men during slavery, worked primarily as domestics. Although most blacks worked as common laborers of one sort or another, some set up small business enterprises or engaged in professional activities. The 1795 city directory listed black grocers, fruiterers, shopkeepers, and milkmen, among others. There were also a few artisans practicing shipbuilding, metal- and leather-working, and other crafts.

The black situation was not idyllic, however, for many worked as servants in white households, much as they had in slavery. This meant, as in slavery, a fractured family life, because few white owners or employers were prepared to keep a whole black family together under one roof. They might be spread throughout the city, or even outside it. Many black youths were indentured—bound by contract to serve others for a specified number of years. This was a practice common with white children as well, but white females normally served until age 18 and white males until 21, whereas blacks usually served until 28. These were their most productive years in a lifespan that did not usually extend much past 40.

One of the first tasks of freed blacks, therefore, was to claim an independent residence. In view of their economic circumstances, this was not always easy, and the move out of white households and into stable two-parent family groupings proceeded by stages. Along the way, blacks sometimes formed extended families, locating several generations under one roof, or made other creative household arrangements in order to remove themselves sooner from the constraints of life in white homes. In Boston, where slavery ended soonest, a majority of blacks lived in two-parent households as early as 1790, and the percentage increased in the 19th century. This was also true in New York City at the same date, but its proportion decreased in the following decades as a result of the expansion of slavery in the city in the 1790s. In Philadelphia, where the emancipation process was slower than in Boston, close to half of blacks lived in two-parent households in 1790 and the process of independent family formation speeded up thereafter. Blacks moved rapidly after slavery to secure a degree of social and cultural independence based on strong families and their own religious outlook.

Perhaps Philadelphia blacks developed confidence in America, despite discrimination, because of their large and growing community and because of significant support from whites. Their most dedicated supporter, Anthony Benezet, died in 1784. But his place was taken somewhat by the physician Benjamin Rush, who gave active backing to the African church project and to other issues of concern to blacks. In addition, the Pennsylvania Society for the Abolition of Slavery was revived in 1784. It found renewed work in preventing the sale or kidnapping of bondspeople to the South, in monitoring other evasions of the manumission law, and in aiding blacks to get employment. The aged Benjamin Franklin lent his prestige by becoming president of the society.

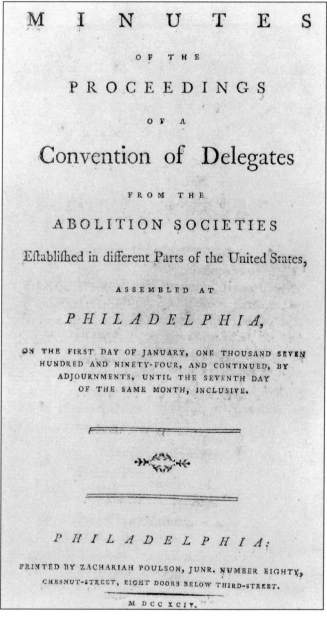

MINUTES

OF THE

PROCEEDINGS

OF A

Convention of Delegates

FROM THE

ABOLITION SOCIETIES

Eſtabliſhed in different Parts of the United States,

ASSEMBLED AT

PHILADELPHIA,

ON THE FIRST DAY OF JANUARY, ONE THOUSAND SEVEN HUNDRED AND NINETY-FOUR, AND CONTINUED, BY ADJOURNMENTS, UNTIL THE SEVENTH DAY OF THE SAME MONTH, INCLUSIVE.

PHILADELPHIA:

PRINTED BY ZACHARIAH POULSON, JUNR. NUMBER EIGHTY, CHESNUT-STREET, EIGHT DOORS BELOW THIRD-STREET.

M DCC XCIV.

Philadelphia's large free black population made it an ideal site for this meeting of delegates from various abolition societies.

The smaller black population in New England, not quite submerged in a sea of whites, apparently lacked similar support and showed signs of having greater disappointment in their white neighbors. Certainly the nature of repressive laws there suggests that conclusion. The experience of Phillis Wheatley also supports it. Despite her celebrity status, she was never able to raise a sufficient number of subscriptions in Boston to permit publication of a second volume of her work. She was reduced, instead, to labor outside her home, doing the kind of difficult domestic work in freedom that she was spared in slavery. She wrote Philadelphia abolitionist John Thornton in 1774, soon after her liberation, to lament that "the World is a severe schoolmaster, for its frowns are far less dang'rous than its smiles and flatteries . . . I attended and find exactly true your thoughts on the behaviour of those who seem'd to respect me while [I was] under my mistresses patronage; you said right, for some of those have already put on a reserve."

The domestic chores of housecleaning, washing, sewing, and cooking, the common lot of black women of the era, were strenuous tasks in the 18th century, and overtaxing to someone of Wheatley's delicate physique. She was probably also undernourished, for her marriage to free black John Peters in 1778 was not entirely successful. He was apparently overproud and unable to provide for her as well as she could have wished. She was reported at one stage to be living in abject poverty. None of her three children survived. She was only 31 years old when she died at the end of 1784.

While Northern blacks moved toward greater self-definition, southern blacks did the same. They operated under greater restraints than simple racism, however, for most were still enslaved. Although the religious revivals of the Great Awakening left the mass of slaves unaffected, they appealed to blacks nevertheless. African Americans responded particularly to the doctrine resolved by a Baptist committee in 1789 that slavery was "a violent deprivation of the rights of nature, and inconsistent with a republican government." By the 1770s, a number of blacks had been converted by Baptist or Methodist preachers and felt the call to go out on their own. If they were slaves, they sometimes left without permission, as runaway ads in newspapers testify. Virginia-born Primus, who left his master in 1772 when he was "about nineteen or twenty Years of Age," had "been a Preacher ever since he was sixteen." He had "done much Mischief in his Neighborhood." Nat, who "pretends to be very religious, and is a Baptist teacher," left home in 1778. They were followed five years later by Tim, "about thirty," who had "a very smooth way of speaking" and was "a Baptist preacher."

These men, about whom we know nothing more, were joined by other black Baptists who left greater account of themselves and were responsible for setting up Baptist churches in Virginia, South Carolina, and elsewhere. Such men were involved in the first black Baptist church in America developed independently of a white one. It was started in Silver Bluff, South Carolina, between 1773 and 1775. From this region, including nearby Savannah, Georgia, came a band of black Baptists who went on to found separate black churches in various parts of the world.

George Liele has been described as the Southern (and Baptist) counterpart of Richard Allen and as the energy behind the early black churches in Georgia and South Carolina. Born in Virginia, he accompanied his master to Savannah, Georgia. His master was a loyalist who freed Liele before his death in British service in 1778. Liele, meanwhile, preached to slaves on plantations along the Savannah River and moved into the city of Savannah after his master's demise. There he continued to preach to slaves and he brought the future preacher Andrew Bryan to the faith. Liele left with the British, however, unsure of his free status without their protection, and introduced the Baptist church to Jamaica.

Still a slave, Andrew Bryan refused to depart with the others who cast their lot with the English; he ministered to a small congregation in Savannah instead. In the period of unrest at the end of the war, however, they were persecuted by anxious whites and Bryan had to suffer for his faith. He and his brother "were twice imprisoned, and about *fifty* were severely whipped, particularly *Andrew, who was cut, and bled abundantly,*" a fellow minister revealed in a letter. But Bryan "told his persecutors that he rejoiced not only to be whipped, but *would freely suffer death for the cause of Jesus Christ*." This willingness to suffer for his beliefs so impressed local officials that he was permitted to resume services, but only between sunrise and sunset. His master even provided a place of worship. In 1788 Bryan was formally licensed to preach, eventually gained his freedom, and by the turn of the century was able to report that the First African Baptist Church of Savannah met "with the approbation and encouragement of many of the white people." The response to his message was so great that two other black Baptist churches soon formed in the city. In 1793, meanwhile, the Silver Bluff church, having outgrown its location, moved 12 miles away to Augusta, Georgia, to form the First African Baptist Church under one of the original founders, Jesse Galpin.

Slaves who preached, and the bound congregations to whom they ministered, had to operate within limitations set by their masters. Like the Methodists, many early Baptist congregations were integrated, even though blacks were normally restricted to a section of their own in the back or balcony. In rural areas, slaves often accompanied their masters to church. Blacks could preach to whites, and vice versa, but blacks usually preached to their own. Though many black churches came into being as a result of independent black activity, others were offshoots of white congregations. Unlike in the North, the move had to be one with which white people agreed, for the activities of enslaved blacks were strictly controlled. Frequently the move to separate came from white people, once the black membership became too large. Blacks might continue to operate on their own, much as they had before, under either a black or white minister, though most preferred a person of their own color, for the message in its subtleties and the preaching style would differ. They would remain under the watchful eye of whites in any case.

Baptist principles of congregational independence made this arrangement easier. Unlike the Methodists, Baptist churches were less subject to the control of a national church organization. They seemed more willing to accept black preachers and allowed more individual freedom. Although they possessed the same beliefs in the equality of all persons as the Methodists did, their lack of structure before the 19th century permitted individuals to accommodate a proslavery message earlier than the Methodists, without it having the same import. While Methodist convocations adopted antislavery policies several times in the 1780s, they had to back off because of popular opposition. Baptist declarations of that kind had not the same organizational support because the congregations were not so tightly bound together or used to taking orders from a national authority. There was no organizational decision on the matter. This permitted individual congregations to adjust to local sentiment without compromising a national decision or obligating other localities. In any case, blacks were early attracted to the denomination, which seemed to have the greatest appeal.

Things changed in the 19th century, when the Baptists, too, desired greater conformity among their members, and, under pressure from secular authorities, withdrew the freedom granted Southern black Baptists. In the meantime, blacks often had significant leeway in choosing their ministers, church officers, and even in sending representatives to regional Baptist associations. The transition can be seen, particularly in the hardening of racial lines, in two decisions of the Baptist Association of Portsmouth, Virginia. In 1794 the association answered the question "Is it agreeable to the Word of God to send a free black man a delegate to the Ass'n?" in the affirmative: "We can see nothing wrong in this. A church may send any one it chooses." In 1828, it decided that "whereas the constitution of independent and colored churches, in this state, and their representation in this body, involves a point of great delicacy," black churches could only be represented by whites.

Southern (and Northern) black Methodists had to fight to obtain the sort of independence enjoyed by Southern black Baptists. The Methodists' personal slights pushed them towards it, however, and blacks in Baltimore, under Daniel Coker, in Wilmington, Delaware, under Peter Spencer, and in other locations departed congregations dominated by white Methodists and eventually joined with Richard Allen to form the African Methodist denomination or made other provisions. Some blacks had to act alone. Sam, who left his Maryland master in 1793, had been "raised in a family of religious persons, commonly called Methodists, and has lived with some of them for years past on terms of perfect equality," an ad for a runaway noted. He left because of a "refusal to continue him on these terms." He had "been in the use of instructing and exhorting his fellow creatures of all colors in matters of religious duty" and may well have continued the practice on his own. A harbinger of more repressive times can be found in the special edition of the Church's *Discipline* for Southern states in 1804 and 1808 (containing religious doctrines and beliefs), which omitted any reference to resolutions on slavery. Even Methodist Bishop Francis Asbury, an early leader of the church who abhorred slavery, eventually gave way before proslavery forces and wrote in his journal that it was more important to save the African's soul than to free his body. But not many African Americans were prepared to accept that priority. Increasingly, in the 19th century, they decided to worship apart from their white brethren.

That was true, of course, when they engaged in Christian worship at all. For important as Christianity was in fostering a will toward independence among blacks, in providing a gauge and a focus for greater self-assertion and self-reliance, in providing solace during times of deprivation, the likelihood is that most blacks were barely touched by it. One historian argues, in fact, that the slaves' religious practices were overwhelmingly more African than Christian. If slave preachers could not relate to those in a plantation community who knew little or nothing about Christianity, he suggests, they could not minister to most of their people. He and other historians push this argument into the 19th century. But it has particular relevance for the 18th century, and especially in the postrevolutionary period, for the number of Africans imported into South Carolina and Georgia exceeded 100,000 before the overseas slave trade finally ended in 1808. These imports brought renewed contact with Africa. But coastal South Carolina and Georgia had maintained a greater African presence than the Chesapeake had anyway, and African-American Christianity, there and elsewhere, was greatly influenced by African beliefs and attitudes. Most prominent is the "ring shout," a counterclockwise circular dance motion accompanied by singing and hand-clapping, which is a basic feature of low country Christianity in South Carolina and Georgia and is argued by several scholars to be essentially African. Yet Christianity developed an increasing appeal to African Americans in the period just before and after the Revolution and its influence was to grow.

PAUL

CAPTAIN

CUFFEE

1812.

ENGRAVED FOR ABRM. L. PENNOCK, BY MASON & MAAS.

CHAPTER 6

PAUL CUFFE AND THE FAILURE OF FREEDOM

◇ ◇ ◇

This 1812 engraving shows Captain Paul Cuffe, a New England merchant-sailor who developed trading interests in Africa and transported black colonists there in 1815.

Despite the religious and, in the Upper South, secular feeling of generosity on the part of whites that made life more tolerable for blacks in the decade after the American revolution, planters renewed their commitment to black bondage. In most cases, indeed, it scarcely slackened. Although the Lower South was not as affected by the abolitionist trend of the times as regions farther north, it was not completely exempt either. The military proposals of John Laurens, to arm slaves and free them at the war's conclusion, were just one example. A few slaveowners were even moved to manumission. South Carolinian John Peronneau freed his slave Romeo in 1781 "in consequence of my aversion to and abhorrence of Slavery which natural Religion and common sense do equally condemn."

But most Southern whites did not go that far. A Georgia planter readily admitted that racial slavery was "subversive of every idea of moral as well as political justice." He was not prepared to concede that emancipation was the answer, however; rather, he believed that American slaves were better off than European peasants. One historian of South Carolina argues, in fact, that low country planters felt a need to justify slavery even before the revolution, and that this need developed out of an increased recognition of their slaves' humanity. This realization arose partly from the slaves' development of a creole, or American, culture in the second half of the 18th century. Creole originally referred to Europeans born in the New World but now extends to other peoples and things brought to life in the Americas, including culture—for example, language, religion, and new tastes in food. Despite the continued importance of the slave trade to low country planters, by 1760 less than half of South Carolina's slave population was African-born. Creole slaves were closer to their masters in culture and, unlike Africans, were better able to impress upon European-centered white people that they were human beings.

In both regions of the South, a relatively stable, family-based, creole slave society had developed by 1770. In both regions, the slave population had begun to reproduce itself naturally, a clear advantage for planters who maintained family units on their estates. Natural reproduction was greater and more important in the larger and older slave society in the Chesapeake, but its value was also acknowledged farther south. War disrupted this not quite idyllic setting. Slaves were moved and families and communities torn asunder. This process continued in the war's aftermath and was accelerated by economic change.

Cotton was the crop that dominated the plantation economy of the 19th-century South—the South of myth and legend. Eli Whitney's improved cotton gin of 1793, which more easily separated the seeds from the strands of cotton, and is often blamed for perpetuating slavery in a region that expected rapidly to eradicate it, has been unfairly charged. The regions into which cotton expanded so quickly had been preparing for years, and frontier planters needed only the right circumstances to seize their expected promise. But Eli Whitney did make that expansion more certain. Slaves who could clean one pound of cotton in a day without Whitney's invention could prepare 50 pounds with it. The economic possibilities were obvious; production that had formerly been confined to home use could now be grown for commercial export.

In the Lower South, slaves produced cotton independently during the unrest and disorder of revolution and planters made concessions to ensure that they remained on the plantation. Both needed a domestic source of cloth, because imports of all kinds were cut off by British military activity. There was likewise more production of food crops for local consumption than before the war. For planters, the production of cotton and the wearing of local homespun woven from it became a patriotic duty, symbolic of their ability to do without British finery.

But slaves who did not leave the plantation had a personal interest in this cultivation, too, for their well-being, perhaps even more than

By making the production of cotton much more efficient, the cotton gin greatly increased the profit- ability of cotton and increased the demand for slaves throughout the South.

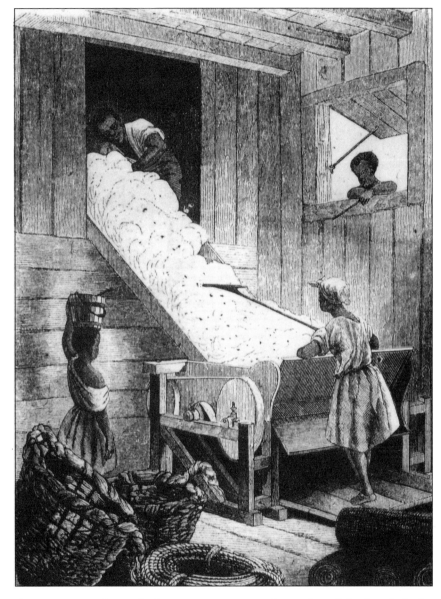

their masters', depended upon it. Many simply produced food and cloth for their own use. Planters were happy to leave them to their own de- vices, so long as they remained on the land. If slaves could extract greater leeway from their owners to grow something they needed any- way, so much the better. But, as one historian keenly advises, there was a depressing irony in this situation of wartime independence. The crop that provided slaves a temporary liberation from the master's stern gaze during the Revolution formed the links of a chain that more tightly bound their children and grandchildren.

Low country planters continued to grow rice, both during and after the revolution, but the industry was undergoing a transition to a new method of cultivation using the tidal flow from rivers. This process required an initial output of tremendous labor to construct embankments, dig ditches, and build "trunks" or sluices (water passages) to control the flow of water onto the rice fields. It saved labor in cultivation, particularly in terms of weeding, but required considerable maintenance.

Indigo, which had supplemented rice cultivation in the colonial period, was replaced after the Revolution by cotton. As with indigo, slaves attended to cotton during the periods when the rice fields needed less attention. A long-staple variety, called sea island cotton, suitable to warm, moist conditions, grew along the Georgia–South Carolina seacoast and on islands off the coast. Short-staple varieties spread inland into the piedmont and backcountry of South Carolina and Georgia, across the dark, fertile soils of Florida, Mississippi, Alabama, and Louisiana, and up over the Appalachians and Alleghenies into Kentucky and Tennessee. They penetrated the Virginia frontier and various locations in the Chesapeake. It was the spread of these short-staple varieties that Whitney's gin aided, for the seed separated more easily from long-staple cotton.

The spread of cotton affected African-American communities all along the eastern seaboard. The greater freedom that war had brought to slaves in most regions continued for some time thereafter, though more in some places than others. In the Chesapeake Bay area, slaves experienced more mobility, greater access to freedom, and more opportunity for employment and self-improvement once freedom came. Some planters, particularly in Maryland, freed their slaves and set them up as tenants. Other recently-freed blacks began a slow process of setting themselves up independently.

However, as the Chesapeake area's major crop, tobacco, decreased in price, many slaveholders decided to sell their slaves to buyers in the booming markets of the southwest, or else move there themselves with their slaves. Between 1790 and 1810, 100,000 slaves were moved from the Chesapeake Bay area into newly opening cotton lands in the West and Southwest. Communities were ruptured and families dissolved as slaves accompanied masters toward a white man's opportunity. In their new locales, they had to begin the painful process of reconstructing fam-

TO BE SOLD, on board the Ship *Bance-Island*, on tuefday the 6th of *May* next, at *Afhley-Ferry*; a choice cargo of about 250 fine healthy NEGROES, juft arrived from the Windward & Rice Coaft. —The utmoft care has already been taken, and fhall be continued, to keep them free from the leaft danger of being infected with the SMALL-POX, no boat having been on board, and all other communication with people from *Charles-Town* prevented.

Auftin, Laurens, & Appleby.

N. B. Full one Half of the above Negroes have had the SMALL-POX in their own Country.

An ad for a slave auction to be held aboard ship in the port of Charleston, South Carolina. The majority of slaves imported into 18th-century British North America entered through Charleston.

ily and community in a situation not as advantageous as the ones they had left. In the new regions there were more farms than plantations, few slaves on each unit, long distances between individual landholdings, hard labor in clearing fresh land, and little chance of finding a mate. The erosion of slavery continued in Maryland but, because of cotton, many blacks born there would not stay to see it. They went west to make their masters' fortune.

The frontier clamor for cotton slaves was also met by recourse to the slave trade. At least 100,000 slaves were imported from Africa between 1783 and 1807, and directed to developing cotton regions. This trade entered through Savannah in the 1790s, since South Carolina had suppressed the commerce. In view of the looming constitutional prohibition of the trade, which would take effect in 1808, however, South Carolina belatedly responded to inland settlers and reopened its ports in 1803. Slavers then shifted to Charleston and landed almost 10,000 Africans a year until the final termination of the trade.

Nearly half of these slaves came from the Congo-Angola region of Central Africa, reinforcing a strain of African culture that had predominated in the first decades of the 18th century. People from this region had led the largest slave revolt in colonial British North America and had a reputation for possessing an aptitude for mechanical skills. Another quarter left the Senegambia area of West Africa, fortifying a cultural tradition that had been influential throughout the period. People from this region contributed to the development of South Carolina's rice industry. These new imports were going mostly to different regions than their country people who preceded them, so the cultural effect may not have been as profound as it could have been. Indeed, these Africans were moving where they most likely encountered creole slaves from the Chesapeake. Culturally different, the two groups would have had to forge a common identity as they formed a new community.

Some blacks, who had developed maroon, or runaway, communities during the war refused to give up their freedom after it, and they continued to enjoy greater liberty than a slave society could possibly permit. Thus the *Charleston Morning Post* reported in October 1786 that a group of around 100 African Americans had established an independent settlement on an island in the Savannah River, about 18 miles from the coast. From there they conducted periodic foraging expeditions against neighboring plantations to supplement the supplies they grew. Aside from the threat to landowners in the vicinity, their message of self-assertion was not one that planters desired to see spread. Already their slaves too often went their own way, and this group was not the only example of bondsmen who continued to reject white authority entirely.

The landowners' reaction, as reported, was swift:

> On Wednesday the 11th [of October] a small party of Militia landed and attacked them, and killed three or four, but were at last obliged to retire for want of ammunition, having four of their number wounded. The same evening, near to sunset, fifteen of the Savannah Light Infantry and three or four others drove in one of their out guards, but the Negroes came down in such numbers that it was judged advisable to return to their boats, from which the Negroes attempted to cut them off, but were prevented by Lieutenant Elfe of the artillery, who commanded a boat with 11 of the company, and had a field piece on board, which he discharged three times with grape shot, and it is thought either killed or wounded some of them, as a good deal of blood was afterwards seen about the place to which the shot was directed.

Two days later a larger force attacked the settlement, forced the blacks to retreat, and destroyed their homes, fields, and supplies, along with "14 or 15 boats and canoes. The loss of their provisions," the *Post* reasoned, "will occasion them to disperse about the country, and it is hoped will be the means of most of them being soon taken up." But the threat did not disappear.

Most African Americans, enslaved and free, found other ways to assert their autonomy. This is easiest seen in how they named themselves. Northern blacks who won their freedom frequently took a new name. The names their owners chose from Greek or Roman history or mythology, such as Caesar, Cato, Diana, or Daphne, or from European places such as London or Hanover, were gradually replaced by English or biblical names such as James, John, Elizabeth, or Sarah. Parents with these older names did not pass them along to their children. Commonly, they rejected their previous names themselves, choosing new ones soon after emancipation. The use even of African names diminished, indicating blacks' increasing American identification.

They also took surnames, seldom memorializing past masters. Neither Richard Allen nor Absalom Jones took the names of their former owners. Those who remained in bondage in Southern states claimed the right to name their offspring. They often called their children after relatives, particularly their fathers, from whom sons and daughters might be separated. Accordingly, Thomas Jefferson's slave woman Molly, wife of Phill Waggoner, named their first two children Phill and Phyllis. If their masters insisted on calling them one thing, they might still be known as something else in the quarters, among the common folk with whom they lived and worked. There was more than one way to insist upon their humanity.

While blacks struggled to define themselves, the nation also groped toward an identity. Free blacks in Southern slave society, even more than those in free-labor Northern ones, faced an uncertain situation in a nation in flux. Racial lines were drawn, but not as inflexibly as they would become. For instance, the situation of free colored people in Charleston, often of mixed blood and tied by interest and inclination to the planter class, was not the same as that of free blacks in the Chesapeake area, who were offered little protection by prominent whites and thus fended for themselves. The status of free blacks and coloreds, or mixed-race people, in New Orleans, when it became part of the United States in 1803, was different still. In 1790 Charleston's colored elite formed the Brown Fellowship Society, a mutual benefit organization similar to those formed by Northern blacks. However, it excluded people with darker skins. New Orleans had similar associations. The various regions of the nation and the variants of black culture would move toward greater uniformity in the 19th century. But it would be a mistake to read the present back into the past and to assume that race relations in the 18th century were always worse than in the 20th. The careers of two men, both born free, one (Benjamin Banneker) in a slave society, the other (Paul Cuffe) in one of the earliest free societies that had once tolerated slavery, demonstrate the unformed and still flexible nature of the national atmosphere.

Born in 1731, Benjamin Banneker was the grandson of European and African immigrants, an Englishwoman named Molly Welsh and the African man she bought, freed, and married, called Bannaka. Interracial marriages were illegal in the Maryland of Molly Welsh's day, and she faced the enduring threat of punishment for her transgression. Yet in her life among her husband's people in the countryside outside Baltimore she apparently was not bothered.

Benjamin, whose mother was Molly's daughter and whose father was also a freed slave, grew up in a peaceful setting. He attended a one-room schoolhouse with several white and one or two colored youngsters, taught by a Quaker schoolmaster. The school was open only in the winter, and the rest of the year he had to help his family with the farmwork—raising tobacco and corn, caring for a few cattle and chickens, working in his mother's vegetable garden or his father's orchard, hunting and fishing in nearby woods and streams, and performing other chores that any farmboy who lived in a wilderness environment might have to do. He was more lucky than most, for his parents owned the land they worked and his name was on the deed. He would inherit it. Despite the necessity for physical labor, at an early age he developed an interest in mathematics and, in view of the limitations of his schooling, was largely self-taught.

He first came to local fame when in 1753, at 22 years of age, he built a clock. Modeled after a watch he had borrowed, it was painstakingly constructed nearly all of wood, and illustrated an unusual mechanical genius. It operated until his death more than 50 years later.

Benjamin Banneker was born free in Maryland in 1731 and, among other accomplishments, later helped survey the national capital at Washington, D.C.

During the revolutionary period, when the new nation was deprived of European supplies, more American clockmakers would use local woods in their craft and others would make clocks nearly all of wood. But Banneker was the first to construct a clock using only American materials.

Late in life he added to his interest in horology, the science and art of measuring time and making timepieces, an interest in astronomy, the study of the stars and planets. He borrowed books and instruments from a neighbor and mastered a new science. He went on to publish several popular almanacs and was appointed by Secretary of State Thomas Jefferson to help survey the federal territory for the new national capital at Washington, D.C. He worked with Andrew Ellicott, the chief surveyor, from February to April 1791. He had never before been away from his birthplace. Excited about the project though he was, he was then an old man of 60 years and unaccustomed to the rugged discomfort of wilderness surveying. He was not unhappy to return to his farm when Ellicott secured other aid.

Born free, an owner of land, with a rudimentary education and gifted with uncommon mathematical and mechanical skill, Banneker experienced relatively little discrimination as far as we know. Nor was he much touched by the Revolutionary struggle. The region in which he lived largely escaped military conflict. His was not the typical 18th-century Maryland black experience any more than Phillis Wheatley represented the typical New England slave. This does not mean that he had no knowledge of America's racial divide, for he surely knew that the attention he received derived partly from his color and the assumptions people made about it. Moreover, when white engineers in the District of Columbia "overlooked" his color, as an early commentator described the scene, and invited him to eat with them, "his characteristic modesty" prompted him to decline the offer. He dined in the same tent but at a separate table. This surely tells much about developing racial customs.

Banneker, like Wheatley, was caught up in the abolitionist crusade through the continuing controversy over blacks' intellectual capacities. Accordingly, the *Georgetown Weekly Ledger* described him soon after his arrival in the Federal District as "an Ethiopian, whose abilities, as a surveyor, and an astronomer, clearly prove that Mr. Jefferson's concluding that race of men were void of mental endowments, was without foundation." If Wheatley became the rage of the pre–Revolutionary

Benjamin Bannaker's
PENNSYLVANIA, DELAWARE, MARY-
LAND, AND VIRGINIA
ALMANAC,
FOR THE
YEAR of our LORD 1795;
Being the Third after Leap-Year.

BANNAKER.

—PRINTED FOR—
And Sold by JOHN FISHER, *Stationer.*
BALTIMORE.

The title page from Banneker's Almanac—on which his name was misspelled—from 1795. He sent a manuscript copy of his first almanac to Thomas Jefferson in 1791 in an attempt to discredit ideas about black inferiority.

antislavery set, Banneker became almost as important for the post–Revolutionary generation. In some ways he was more important, for his achievements were scientific rather than literary. Of the latter there were several cases, but examples of the former were rare indeed. If blacks were to gain full rights of citizenship, it was clearly important that they exhibit a broad intellectual competence. With the coming of freedom to the North and the continuing struggle against the Atlantic traffic in slaves, postwar abolitionists sought as much evidence of black talent as they could muster.

Banneker even engaged in an exchange with Jefferson on the issue. Before his first published almanac (which required advanced knowledge in mathematics and astronomy to produce) appeared, he sent a manuscript copy to the secretary of state, noting the general prejudice against blacks and hoping that Jefferson was not of so inflexible a disposition. Jefferson replied promptly, "Nobody wishes more than I do to see such proofs as you exhibit that nature has given to our black brethren talents equal to those of the other colors of men, and that the appearance of the want of them is owing merely to the degraded condition of their existence, both in Africa and America." Jefferson wrote that he desired an end to their subservience "as fast as the imbecility of their present existence, and other circumstances which cannot be neglected, will admit." The "other circumstances" almost certainly referred to white racial prejudice and Jefferson's conviction that blacks must be sent out of the country.

Jefferson sent the almanac to a friend in Paris suggesting that it was evidence of the type needed to disprove Jefferson's own presumption of black inferiority. But he was not convinced. He later expressed doubt that Banneker had done the work himself. He had no reason to imagine that, except an emotional inability to believe that blacks could achieve. Many other whites, equally dubious, were prepared to give way before the evidence. David Rittenhouse, America's foremost astronomer, praised Banneker's work as "a very extraordinary performance," and Maryland statesman James McHenry, like Jefferson a Southerner, considered Banneker as "fresh proof that the powers of the mind are disconnected with the colour of the skin."

Nevertheless, Jefferson was right on the mark in his assessment of the political cost of speaking out on slavery, and when his correspondence with Banneker was published, he came under attack. "What shall we think of a *secretary of state*," Congressman William Loughton Smith of South Carolina wrote in 1796, opposing Jefferson's political aims, "thus fraternizing with negroes, writing them complimentary epistles, stiling them *his black brethren*, congratulating them on the evidences of their *genius*, and assuring them of his good wishes for their speedy emancipation?" So far had the nation moved from the principles of the Revolution that an expression of faith in human equality, however tentatively offered, and a sympathetic word in favor of black freedom, however qualified, could be shaped into a weapon designed to destroy a career. American society was not yet everywhere rigidly stratified in terms of race, but all the attitudes were there.

Curiously, the sort of evidence that the dubious would accept for blacks' vindication was rather limited. Despite the accomplishments of people like Prince Hall, Richard Allen, and Absalom Jones, 18th-century abolitionists never used them as evidence of blacks' intellectual capacity. This was because men of the post–Revolutionary generation, including figures like Benjamin Rush and Thomas Jefferson, separated intellect from morals. Although these two men differed in their judgment of blacks' mental endowments, neither had any doubt about their moral sense or their susceptibility to religion. If blacks acted out of moral outrage, therefore, or from religious motivation, their other successes were not counted in the evaluation of their brain power.

Blacks also demonstrated organizational ability, or capabilities in financial management, but these were seldom brought forward for discussion in considering their intellect. Consequently, the business success of Paul Cuffe—a New England shipping entrepreneur—was not something that abolitionists immediately valued in championing blacks' mental equality. Indeed, if that were his only claim to fame, important though it was, he might be passed over quickly. Yet his career is a measure of what skill mixed with luck could bring about for a black man in early America and is an answer to American racism of that era. It is also a cautionary tale of how and why a black man of the time could become disillusioned with America's promise.

When Cuffe came to the attention of the Delaware Society for the Abolition of Slavery as a result of business connections, the society published a short biographical tract. The purpose of this pamphlet, which was published in 1807, was to prove that

Banneker published his almanac yearly from 1792 to 1797 and completed manuscript copies to 1802, some of which may also have been published. Abolitionists used his accomplishments as important evidence that African Americans were intelligent enough to care for themselves in freedom.

PREFACE.

GENTLE READER,

To make an ALMANAC is not so easy a matter as some people think—like a well furnished table it requires to have a variety of dishes to suit every palate, besides considerable skill in the cooking—Now as it is impossible to suit all the dishes to every particular taste, we hope you will not be offended, should you find any not entirely to your liking as we are certain there are a great many which will suit you to a hair. We are persuaded you will not only be entertained but instructed by our Almanac. for we have ransacked all the repositories of learning to cull a few flowers for your amusement. Moreover, Kind Reader, as we believe you would think the better of a man for having a decent coat on his back, so we have exerted ourselves to make our Almanac appear in a more respectable dress, than some other Almanac mongers have done, who, it would seem, have thought their Almanacs not worthy a good coat.

But there is one dish we invite you to partake of, and we are prouder of it than of all the rest put together; and to whom do you think are we indebted for this part of our entertainment? Why, to a Black Man—Strange! Is a Black capable of composing an Almanac? Indeed it is no less strange than true; and a clever, wise, long headed Black he is: It would be telling some whites if they had made as much use of their great school learning, as this sage philosopher has made of the little teaching he has got.

The labours of the justly celebrated Bannaker will likewise furnish you with a very important lesson courteous reader, which you will not find in any other Almanac. namely, that the Maker of the Universe is no respecter of colours; that the colour of the skin is no ways connected with strength of mind or intellectual powers; that although the God of Nature has marked the face of the African with a darker shade than his brethren, he has given him a soul equally capable of refinement. To the untutored Blacks the following elegant lines of GRAY may be applied.

" Full many a gem of purest ray serene,
" The dark unfathom'd caves of ocean bear:
" Full many a flower is borne to blush unseen,
" And waste its fragrance on the desert air."

Nor you ye proud, impute to these the blame
If Afric's sons to genius are unknown,
For Bannaker has prov'd they may acquire a name
As bright, as lasting as your own.

with suitable culture and a fair opening for the exertion of talents, the NEGRO possesses a portion of intellect and energy by which he is enabled to form great designs, to adopt means to the end in the prosecution of them, to combat danger, to surmount difficulties; and thus to evince that, with equal advantages of education and circumstances, the Negro–race might fairly be compared with their white brethren on any part of the globe.

The society wanted Cuffe to work with Quaker-dominated international antislavery interests in securing black settlements in Africa and it was important for them to show that black people were capable of enterprise. People concerned in the Sierra Leone venture took especial note.

Cuffe's father, Kofi, lived in the Asante kingdom among Akan-speaking peoples on the western coast of Africa. He came to America as part of the slave traffic in 1728 when he was 11 or 12 years old. To his good fortune, he was purchased by a Quaker family, one that evidently had antislavery leanings, and his owner, John Slocum, freed him in 1740. In 1746 he married Ruth Moses, a Wampanoag, and eventually bought a farm on the Massachusetts coast near Martha's Vineyard. Paul was born in 1759, the seventh child and youngest son of ten children. As a farm boy, he, like Banneker, was brought up to hard work and his education was limited. He was largely self-taught but extremely shrewd. His natural charm and native intelligence made up for what he lacked in formal education.

Paul Cuffe's father, Kofi, was brought to this country as a slave in 1728. He was granted his freedom in 1740 and went on to marry and raise 10 children. He kept track of important family events in this notebook.

Cuffe was 13 years old when his father died, and he assumed part of the responsibility of supporting his mother and younger sisters. He did not see his future in farming, however, and like many New Englanders turned to the sea. His skill as a seaman together with his daring as an entrepreneur led eventually to his acquisition of a respectable fleet of ships. Some of these he built himself in his own shipyard. He achieved wealth and popularity and was the most successful black businessman in America at the turn of the 19th century.

Cuffe's success was not without difficulties, however. He was twice attacked by pirates and had all his goods stolen at the beginning of his business career. Only dogged persistence enabled him to continue in his chosen vocation. Once established, he normally traveled with an all-black or a mixed black and Native American crew and was a constant source of amazement. In 1793 he went on a whaling voyage off the coast of Newfoundland and ran into other ships who refused the common custom of cooperating with him in the whale hunt. As a newspaper related the story: "In this emergency Paul resolved to prosecute his under–taking alone, till at length the other vessels thought it most prudent to accede to the usual practice: as they apprehended, his crew . . . might alarm and drive the whales from their reach, and thus defeat their voyages." The black captain and his crew proved their worth; of the seven whales taken by the cooperative fleet, Cuffe's ship took six. Cuffe killed two of these himself.

A compass used by Paul Cuffe. His skill as a seaman helped him to acquire a respectable fleet of ships.

Unlike Banneker, who spent most of his life near his birthplace and was consequently somewhat shielded from racial discrimination, Cuffe traveled widely, which brought him face to face with it. This was particularly the case since he frequently traveled to plantation regions. Many slave societies regarded free blacks with suspicion and unease, none more so than the United States. The divide between slave and free states, however, did not necessarily mark a division in the treatment of free blacks, and Cuffe occasionally experienced racial slights in restaurants or on public transportation in the North as well as the South. Both Maryland and Massachusetts had laws against interracial marriages in the latter half of the 1780s (though Pennsylvania did not). Both Maryland and Massachusetts had repressive legislation aimed at unfamiliar free blacks in the 1790s, though neither state may have strongly enforced it. Repressive laws, whether enforced or not, and racial discrimination, whether constant or not, created an environment that reminded Cuffe of his racial status.

In 1780, when he was 21, Cuffe joined with six other free blacks from his town to present this petition to the state legislature in Boston, protesting the fact that they were forced to pay taxes yet were denied the right to vote.

As a wealthy man, and as one who had started with little and achieved much, he was personally popular. Moreover, he was generous. He and his wife had two sons and six daughters; in 1797 he purchased a farm for them in Westport, Massachusetts, and soon became the town's most wealthy citizen. Concerned about the education of his children, he proposed to the townspeople that they get together and build a schoolhouse, as there was none in the area. When they refused, he built one of his own, on his own property. The townspeople proved perfectly willing to accept its use, once it was constructed. But none of this protected him from discrimination.

Because of his mother and his wife, he remained aware of both his African and Native American heritages. In his protests against discriminatory taxation laws applied against him and his family in the 1770s and 1780s, therefore, he was prepared to use whatever facet of his background that seemed the most favorable.

Cuffe's personal journal is filled with his sketches of ships and buildings, along with his business ideas.

In one petition he said that "we being chiefly of the African extraction" were subject to taxation without representation. In another he said that he and his brother were "Indian men and by law not subject of taxation." Increasingly, however, he identified himself with Africans, and as the 19th century dawned and racial attitudes hardened, his own attitudes hardened as well.

An acquaintance described Cuffe in 1806 as "averse to all mixtures," despite his own marriage across racial and ethnic lines. When his wealth and accomplishments brought white friends to his home, he served them at separate tables. He, like Banneker, "reluctantly partook of vituals with persons of other colors." The fact that this attitude developed as a result of unequal treatment is indicated by his observation to the acquaintance that "he would willingly consent to be skinned if his black could be replaced by white." He was increasingly drawn to the conclusion that black people might be better off in Africa, and he became a leading figure in 19th-century emigrationist projects. Although he carried a group of black people there in 1815, he never actually committed to moving to Africa himself. Certainly his wife had no interest in going, and perhaps his children did not either. Besides, whether they went there or not, many black Americans by that time looked with interest at the prospect of black nation-building much closer to home.

CHAPTER 7
HAITI AND THE IMAGE OF FREEDOM

◇ ◇ ◇

Haitian patriot Toussaint Louverture (right) became the most important military leader during the first stage of the Haitian Revolution.

P rince Hall, the founder of African-American freemasonry, addressed his African Lodge in Cambridge, Massachusetts, in June 1797 concerning racial harassment directed at black Americans in public places in Boston. Ten years had passed since the arrival of the charter from England granting them formal recognition as a lodge, and various proposals for blacks to leave America to escape discrimination had failed. But the negative attitudes that had prevented black Masons from gaining a local charter, and caused some blacks to want to leave their homeland for an uncertain future overseas, were alive and well.

Indeed, in many areas of the United States they were stronger. The revolutionary current favorable to black freedom in the South had reversed itself and abolition had not yet succeeded in New York and New Jersey. Hall advised his brethren to be mindful of "these numerous sons and daughters of distress" yet enslaved and who, of all the downtrodden peoples on the earth, deserved their particular consideration. He also charged them to have patience and forbearance in face of the "daily insults we meet with in the streets of Boston," especially on "public days of recreation." He went on to describe vividly how envious white working men and women, some not long out of servitude themselves (for some had come indentured—bound to serve their masters for a period of years before living on their own), and doubtless encouraged by alcoholic beverages imbibed to enliven the holiday, "shamefully abused" blacks who ventured upon the parks or public squares. "[A]t such times," he lamented, ". . . we may truly be said to carry our lives in our hands. . . .

Helpless women have [had] their clothes torn from their backs." Nevertheless, Hall had hopes for change. He cast his eyes with expectation to the Caribbean where, a few years earlier, in response to revolution in France, enslaved men and women in the French Empire had staked their own claim to freedom. "[S]ix years ago, in the French West Indies," Hall related, "Nothing but the snap of the whip was heard, from morning to evening. . . . But, blessed be God, the scene is changed. They now confess that God hath no respect of persons."

At the time that Hall spoke, slavery had been abolished in the French colonies in the Caribbean, the most important of which were Saint Domingue, Guadaloupe, and Martinique. Moreover, under the French revolutionary slogan of "Liberty, Equality, and Fraternity," revolutionary patriots were attempting to construct interracial societies consistent with their beliefs. In Saint Domingue this process went farther and lasted longer than anyplace else. In 1797 the black liberator Toussaint Louverture was well on the way to establishing his leadership over the colony. He had already made clear his disposition to build a society where people of all colors could live in peace and prosperity. He had also left no doubt of his determination that freedom, seized by force of arms, would not be easily surrendered. Although his vision of interracial cooperation was ultimately to fade amid bloody strife, he led the only successful slave revolution in the history of the world. And the banner of black freedom he raised was to stand as a beacon to black men and women throughout the Americas. Its example would spur unrest and insurrection from Brazil to the United States. Its triumph would provide lingering inspiration.

There had been many slave revolts before, and there would be many thereafter. As long as slavery existed there was violent resistance to it. Slaves sometimes escaped and formed maroon (runaway) communities where they lived outside the slave system. In many parts of the Americas these black rebels fought their masters to a standstill and forced a recognition of their individual freedom. They often received arms and supplies in return for their promise not to disturb the plantations. But never before, not even in the ancient world, had slaves ever overthrown and restructured an entire slave society. Although the United States was the first nation in the Americas to achieve its independence, Haiti was the second. And though the United States was the first to de-

A 19th-century engraving entitled Pacification with the Maroon Negroes. *The British tried unsuccessfully to occupy Haiti in the 1790s because they viewed an independent black nation there as a threat to their own slave empire in the Caribbean.*

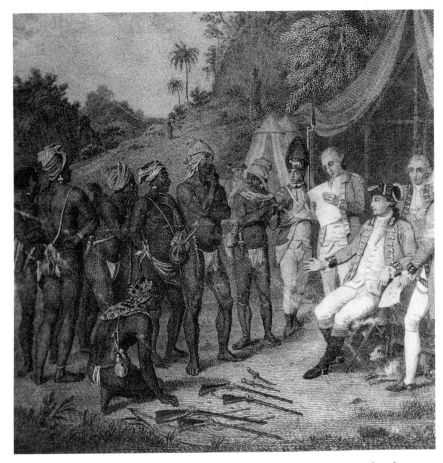

clare that all men were created equal, Haiti was the first to make that declaration a fact.

The Haitian Revolution was the third in a series of democratic revolutions that changed the way people in the Western world viewed government, society, politics, and individual freedom. The era is often called the Age of Revolution. Each was more radical and far-reaching than the previous one, and each expanded the limits of ideas expressed in the Enlightenment.

The American Revolution was the first of the three. It was conceived as a political rather than a social revolution (that is, it sought to change the government rather than the everyday lives of the people), although it laid the basis of a social revolution. Moreover, it had some immediate social consequences, including the Northern abolition of slavery. These consequences were constrained, however, by the conservative nature of its aristocratic and middle-class leaders, who did not want the world as they knew it totally altered.

The French Revolution was the second uprising in the Western world. It was a social as well as a political revolution, for it accomplished not just the displacement but the overturning and destruction of the French monarchy and much of the nobility and a reordering of French government and society. The most radical of its participants sought the absolute ruin of the former ruling classes. The shock waves of revolution in France extended to the colony on Saint Domingue. There it established principles of individual liberty beyond the dreams even of most of the revolutionary generation in North America, and of many in France itself.

One essential feature of the American Revolution was that ordinary people came to believe that no one was essentially better than anyone else. This was a concept of equality that existed in no European nation. But it was a belief marred by a racial divide. It did not extend to people of color, except among the most forward-looking Americans. It did not even extend to white women. The foundation for an expansion of the American idea of liberty was expressed in the Declaration of Independence, and many people recognized the significance. The French were the first Europeans to accept the implications, although they did so by stages. Even they wavered on the issue of color. The force of events as much as the thrust of revolutionary logic led to the abolition of slavery in the French Empire in 1794. While the French advanced, Americans retreated, and by the end of the century they slowly withdrew from the most liberal interpretations of their political statements. It was left to former slaves in Haiti to found a lasting citizenship that included people of color.

The American Revolution influenced the succeeding French upheaval in several ways. The ideals expressed to justify American political separation from Great Britain were based partly on French Enlightenment ideas and appealed to many people in France. Frenchmen like the Marquis de Lafayette served in the American Revolutionary War. For diplomatic reasons, the French government also came to America's defense. But the economic and military aid the French supplied Americans cost more than the French government could afford and caused the French king, Louis XVI, to call together an assembly to reorganize the government. The assembly consisted of representatives from the three classes that composed French society: the First Estate, or the church; the Second Estate, or the nobility; and the Third Estate, or all the rest of the people. The Third Estate, encouraged by popular unrest, decided in 1789 that it ought to represent the French people as a whole and that French society needed to be reformed to allow more equality in its political system.

In June 1789 the Third Estate designated itself the National Assembly and invited members of the other estates interested in reform to join with it. The principles justifying these aims were expressed in the Declaration of the Rights of Man and Citizen, adopted by the assembly on August 27. It, like the American Declaration of Independence, was a statement of universal truths and human rights based on Enlightenment thought. And, like the American declaration, it proclaimed human equality, the right of rebellion, and the sanctity of property. Both documents derived from the writings of Enlightenment thinkers like the English philosopher John Locke, whose second *Treatise of Civil Government* (1690) outlined the theory of limited government.

Locke advanced what was called a liberal theory of government, one primarily concerned with maintaining individual rights and reducing government to the minimum necessary to preserve personal freedom and safety. French philosopher Jean Jacques Rousseau's democratic theory of government, by contrast, placed more emphasis on popular rule than individual rights. When people in a state of nature realized the need to combine in a civil community for the common welfare, they gave up their individual political yearnings to the general will. What the majority decided governed, and there was no individual right except through reasoned discussion to influence opinion. Rousseau published these ideas in the *Discourse on the Origin of Inequality* (1755) and *The Social Contract* (1762).

The French Revolution was at first dominated by moderates whose views were much like those of American revolutionaries such as John Adams, George Washington, and Thomas Jefferson. Soon, however, more radical groups took over. It was during this stage that the king was beheaded and a republic proclaimed. The final part of the revolution was controlled by a group called the Jacobins, who were the most radical of all. They believed in a centralized government, expansion of the right to vote, and elimination of all traces of the old aristocracy. It was they who achieved the abolition of slavery in 1794.

An 1805 account of the Haitian Revolution included this gruesome illustration with the caption: "Revenge taken by the black army for the cruelties practised on them by the French."

The struggle in Saint Domingue was more bloody than even the French Revolution, because added to the conflicting outlooks and tangle of local interests was the complicating factor of race. Saint Domingue society was also divided into three classes, consisting of whites, free people of color, and slaves. As in North America, and partly under American revolutionary influence, white colonists wanted less restrictive trade regulations. They particularly wanted greater leeway to exchange their goods with New Englanders, on whom they depended for many of their supplies. They also wanted greater say in how they were governed. Revolution in France provided an opportunity to press these aims, but it also posed a threat. As much as they wanted greater freedom for them-selves, they desired no change in island social structure, and in this regard, the most radical principles of the revolution stood against them. The first article of the Declaration of the Rights of Man proclaims that "men are born and remain free and equal in their rights." This is a dangerous principle in a society based on the labor of slaves. Moreover, Saint Domingue's free people of color were subject to severe social and political discrimination and they wanted greater freedom of their own. They saw no problem with maintaining slavery so long as all free people, regardless of color, participated in the government.

The free people of color were supported in France by the Society of the Friends of the Blacks. Too many people in France and the West Indies had too great a stake in slavery and the slave trade for the Friends of the Blacks to stand much chance of succeeding immediately in abolishing these evils. They contented themselves with championing the claims to equality of colonial free people of color. Both they and their opponents saw this as the first step toward a more radical social reconstruction of the colonies. Whites in Saint Domingue therefore rejected the National Assembly's recommendation that a limited number of free coloreds be granted citizenship rights. Consequently, in 1790 the free colored people revolted. The free colored revolt was ruthlessly put down, but the whites also divided among themselves, some favoring a greater degree of local self-rule and separation from France than others. Besides, in the colony, as in France, a few people still preferred royal authority to government reform of any kind. These disputes also led to violence. The divisions among the free classes over the meaning of the revolution provided an opening for the slaves.

The slaves needed no formal declarations, either from Europe or America, to justify their claim to liberty. They greatly outnumbered the white people—indeed, all classes of free people—in Saint Domingue. The vast majority of Saint Dominguan slaves were African-born, had experienced freedom before their captivity, and knew that their subjugation rested on no firmer basis than superior arms. Encouraged by the rumor that the king and National Assembly had decreed three days a week for them to work for themselves and the abolition of whippings, they rose up on August 22, 1791. They would not finally lay down their arms until they proclaimed Haiti an independent nation on January 1, 1804.

The man who soon came to dominate the revolution was Toussaint Louverture. Born in 1744, he was 47 at the start of the rebellion. Of mild disposition, he had been fortunate in his master and had not suffered the severe mistreatment of some slaves. Indeed, by the time of the outbreak, he was free in all but name; aside from the duties of coachman, he lived pretty much on his own, with his wife and three boys. "We went to labor in the field, my wife and I, hand in hand," he would later relate. "Scarcely were we conscious of the fatigue of the day. . . . On the Sabbath and festival days we went to church—my wife, my parents, and myself." He was and remained a devout Catholic. He was also literate, enjoyed reading, and in letters of state composed later made frequent reference to ancient history and philosophy.

Toussaint Louverture was a military genius who also was a brilliant civilian leader.

His fortunate experience was unusual for a region where the face of slavery was particularly harsh, and provided him with a distinctive outlook toward interracial cooperation that set him apart from most people on the island. As a military leader, he was beloved of his men, a strict disciplinarian but willing to share their hardships and to lead by example. Extremely brave in battle, he was wounded 17 times. He was once struck in the mouth by a spent cannon ball but only suffered the loss of some teeth. He had a talent for organization and a genius for warfare. By 1795 he was the colony's leading general and by 1798, with the expulsion of interfering British forces, its effective leader. He defeated French, Spanish, British, and opposing local forces in their turn. He had two abiding aims: to maintain black freedom and to rebuild the island's economy. The first he could do by force of arms; the second with white expertise and cooperation and the controlled labor of free black peasants.

The United States and Great Britain viewed events in Saint Domingue with alarm. Both had slave regions to preserve from the contagion of liberty. The British attempt at conquest as part of its war against France came to naught and when they evacuated, they came to a trade arrangement with Toussaint under which they agreed to supply him in return for his promise not to spread revolution to their territories. The United States was also party to the agreement. President John Adams and the Federalist party he represented had always been pro-

British in the wars between Britain and France that broke out in the wake of the French Revolution. In addition, there had always been strong commercial relations between the French West Indies and New England that continued during the slave rebellion. In the last two years before 1800 the United States and France had engaged in an unofficial naval war that prompted a momentary interruption of commerce with French colonies; but that conflict was soon settled and, in any case, the United States was unwilling to allow the British to monopolize Saint Domingue's trade.

The election of President Thomas Jefferson in 1800 changed the situation. Jefferson was a slaveholder and highly sensitive to the consequences of slave rebelliousness. Moreover, the Democratic-Republican party he led had taken the French side of the European conflict. Napoleon Bonaparte, who had come to power in France, and would soon destroy the First French Republic, wanted to end black rule in Saint Domingue. "How could I grant freedom to Africans," he said, "to uncivilized men who did not even know what a colony was, what France was?" He expected to use force and wanted to deprive the rebels of supplies. Having temporarily made peace with England in 1801, he had little

A model for the relief on the tomb of a French general killed while trying to suppress a revolt in Haiti in 1802.

difficulty convincing that nation and the United States that the eradication of black government was in their best interests. Jefferson was not convinced that Napoleon would succeed in his mission, however, and delayed withdrawing American material support from Toussaint. His decision was further slowed by the news or rumor that Louisiana, recently a colony of Spain, had been transferred to France. Jefferson, like many Americans, looked forward to American expansion into the Louisiana Territory and was convinced that no nation who held that region could long be friends with the United States. He would hedge his bets until he was sure of French intentions. Not until after France agreed to sell Louisiana to the United States in 1803 did Jefferson cease to trade with Saint Domingue.

Part of the reason for Napoleon's decision to sell had to do with the outbreak of war with Britain again and his failure, as Jefferson suspected, to succeed in his conquest of Saint Domingue. Napoleon wanted to rebuild the French Empire, which, under his plan, included restoring slavery. Saint Domingue, once the jewel of French Caribbean possessions, would be restored to its original splendor, and French Louisiana would replace the United States as a supplier of foodstuffs not grown on the island. But he calculated without taking into account the blacks' attachment to their hard-won freedom.

Although he was virtually an independent ruler, Toussaint posed as a defender of the French Republic. The National Convention's law of February 1794 that abolished slavery also made the former slaves French citizens. Toussaint was always careful in his dealings with France to operate as if under the authority of the Republic. He had even resisted British and American pressure to declare Saint Domingue independent in 1798–99 when both nations, one officially, the other unofficially, were at war with France. Conditions changed when France made peace with these English-speaking nations. Under Napoleon's leadership, France now felt strong enough to reassert its control.

Napoleon sent his brother-in-law Charles Leclerc with 16,000 troops in 1802 to "rid us of these gilded Africans," as he ordered, referring to Toussaint and his black generals, "and we shall have nothing more to wish." Once he reasserted French authority, Napoleon planned to remove and banish all black or mulatto officers over the rank of captain in order to put his colonial plan into operation more safely. He thought the colony, deprived of leadership, would keep quiet. Hoping to prevent fanatical resistance at the outset, however, he resorted to deceit and denied any intention of bringing back slavery. "What can you desire," he wrote Toussaint in November 1801, "the freedom of the blacks? You know that in all the countries we have been in, we have given it to the people who had it not." Toussaint was not convinced, and he and his most trusted generals Henri Christophe and Jean Jacques Dessalines resisted.

So long as he posed as a champion of the French promise of liberty, Leclerc had some success. Christophe and Dessalines defected to the French and Toussaint agreed to lay down his arms. But not all rebels surrendered and the colony was still unpacified.

In April 1802 Napoleon reopened the slave trade and nullified the decree abolishing slavery. In June he ordered Leclerc to restore slavery at his discretion. Guadaloupe's governor acted before

Lured to a meeting with the French by the promise of protection, Toussaint was instead arrested and sent to France. He died in a French prison the next year. This engraving from an account of his life shows him saying good-bye to his family before being taken away.

Leclerc, and the arrival of news that slavery had been restored in Guadaloupe and Leclerc's tentative moves in that direction in Saint Domingue aroused the suspicions of more blacks about their future, and more left to join rebel bands. At the same time, Dessalines, in particular, began to play both ends against the middle and lent the rebels secret support. The betrayal of Toussaint, whom the French lured to a June meeting on the promise of protection and then arrested and sent to France, caused outrage. He was to die in prison the next year (April 7, 1803) of suffering from frigid temperatures, bad treatment, and little food. Finally, the increasing brutality of the French spurred resistance. Leclerc decided, in fact, that French control of the island would never be secure until he had destroyed all black men and women over 12 years of age.

But Leclerc, like many of his men, died of yellow fever and was succeeded in November by Count Rochambeau. He was not the best choice. For as Leclerc warned Napoleon, "Rochambeau [is] a brave soldier and a good fighter, [but he] has not an ounce of tact or policy. Furthermore, he has no moral character and is easily led." It was Rochambeau who stood with Washington at the Battle of Yorktown to receive the British surrender. The hero of white revolutionaries in America, however, was the scourge of black revolutionaries in Haiti, and if Dessalines eventually chose to insure Haiti's future by exterminating the whites, Rochambeau led the way when he tried to insure France's future there by exterminating the blacks.

By August 1802 the black generals who had gone over to the French began to desert. In November they held a conference, supported independence, and recognized Dessalines as leader of the resistance. According to legend, Dessalines took the French flag, ripped out the white band, and left a flag of blue and red as the national banner. In 1804, after more months of struggle, the French evacuated and the Republic of Haiti, a name derived from a Native American word for a mountainous place, was proclaimed.

The revolutionary tremors convulsing Saint Domingue troubled the anchors of slavery throughout the Americas. Successive waves of refugees—black, brown, and white—who fled the destructive fighting brought stories both frightful and inspiring to the places where they settled. To Jamaica, Cuba, Louisiana, the Carolinas, Pennsylvania, and New York, to name a few locations, these emigrants took a revolutionary spirit, often modified by a complex mixture of racism and republicanism. Thus a white refugee in Jamaica in 1793 was described as one of "the most violent Democrats imaginable," but was still "an active enemy to the people of Colour," unwilling to permit them any privileges. However a free black shipped to prison in Cuba at about the same time declared himself to be a "good republican," but was yet the "enemy . . . of all whites." For white authorities, the black man was clearly a greater threat than the white man, but either could spark unrest.

From Venezuela to Virginia slaves were encouraged anew to reclaim their natural rights. The Spanish governor of Cuba informed his superiors in 1794, at the height of Jacobin radicalism, that "the rumor is too widespread that the French desire that there be no slaves" and were determined to free them. In 1795 slaves mounted uprisings under French revolutionary influence, reminiscent of Saint Domingue, in Dutch Curaçao; Coro, Venezuela; and Pointe Coupee, Louisiana. In Pointe Coupee, a Frenchmen reported, the rebellion started after a new immigrant "represented how happy those [blacks] of San Domingo were." The governor of Trinidad objected in 1796 to the activities of French seamen in his island, most of whom were "mulattoes and blacks, many of whom have been slaves" and "their conversations and discussions, although unsophisticated, are not so much so that they are not effective in perverting the ideas of our" bondmen.

What happened in Trinidad and elsewhere also happened in the United States and plots and rebellions or rumors of plots and rebellions occurred along the eastern seaboard during the 1790s and later. Whites in Charleston, South Carolina, blamed a series of fires in the city on a group of "French Negroes" who "intended to make a St. Domingo business of it." The next year (1797) white Charlestonians executed three black men accused of starting fires with a view toward revolution. These blacks were likewise from Saint Domingue. Whites overheard two slaves in Richmond, Virginia, planning in 1793 to "kill the white people soon in this place," following the example of blacks "in the French Island."

The most serious threat also occurred in Richmond where, in 1800, the slave Gabriel planned a large-scale uprising. Born on a plantation outside the city in 1776, Gabriel was raised as a blacksmith and taught to read. He grew up in a period of revolutionary ferment and could not avoid being influenced by talk about the rights of man. As a skilled worker he was often hired out and spent much time among working-class people where blacks and whites mixed freely. He, like others, learned about the events in Saint Domingue and that was clearly one source of stimulation. He planned not a war against the whites but a war against the merchants. He expected working-class whites as well as slaves to join his rebellion and warned his followers to spare all "Quakers, the Methodists, and Frenchmen" because of "their being friendly to liberty." He planned to take Richmond and set up a new social and political order, though precisely what kind he did not say. However, he clearly envisioned personal freedom and racial and social equality.

Gabriel's conspiracy was widespread, including people in 10 counties, a few whites among them. He estimated "his associates to the

This picture of "Free Natives of Dominica" offers a glimpse of how some of the wealthy free people of color in St. Domingue may have looked before the Haitian Revolution.

number of 5-600." While not all of these were people he could count on, at least 150 gathered for word of the outbreak. Torrential rains prevented the plan from going into effect on the night it was scheduled and the plot was discovered before it could be reorganized. Gabriel and scores of slaves were hung and others were sold out of the state. But the governor of Virginia, James Monroe, and the vice president of the United States, Thomas Jefferson, could take little comfort in hanging revolutionaries, even black ones. "The other states and the world at large will forever condemn us," Jefferson wrote Monroe, "if we indulge a principle of revenge, or go one step beyond absolute necessity. They cannot lose sight of the rights of the two parties, and the object of the unsuccessful one."

Free blacks as well as slaves were attracted by French principles and the Haitian example of equality. Consequently, a free person of color in New Orleans in 1790 wrote a friend to say, in words that recalled those of Prince Hall in Boston:

> We have the title of "Citizen" in Saint–Domingue. [There] we may speak openly, just as any white person, and can possess the same rank. And do we have any of this under the present [Spanish] government? No sir—and it is unjust. All of us being human, there should be no differences: color should not differentiate us.

Free African Americans in the United States had even more reason to protest, for they lived in a country that boasted of its freedoms but increasingly denied them to former slaves. By the date of Haiti's independence in 1804, slavery was finally on the road to extinction in all the Northern states. At the same time, probably a larger number of slaves had been freed in the South by a master's personal act of conscience than by Northern legislative acts of emancipation. But also by that date racial lines had hardened.

In Virginia, for example, the legislature had once supported education for free blacks; in 1806 it reversed that decision and also denied them the right to carry firearms. Maryland's constitution of 1776 had made the possession of property rather than white skin the requirement for voting. In 1783 the state decided that no blacks freed after that date could vote, hold office, or testify against white people in a court of law, nor could any of their descendants. In 1810 it limited the vote to white men. In Philadelphia it had been customary for many years for black and white people to gather before Independence Hall on the Fourth of July to celebrate the birth of a new nation dedicated to freedom and opportunity. In 1805 the white people drove the black people away. Thereafter blacks approached the festival only at the risk of their lives. Throughout the nation similar events heralded a new birth of intolerance. American democracy, they said, would be limited to white people.

In these circumstances Haiti stood out as a beacon of liberty to oppressed people of color all over the New World. For some, it promised a haven where black people could go and be accorded unqualified rights of citizenship. For most, it showed that any people might secure the blessings of liberty, equality, and brotherhood wherever they were willing to fight for them. It justified the claim that all men were born free and equal and that the desire for liberty burnt in every breast. Most importantly, it supported a belief that history and the force of reason was on their side.

EPILOGUE

◇ ◇ ◇

A momentous period of revolution, born in great hopes for human equality, had ended by 1804 in considerable disillusionment for people of
color. Success in Haiti offered some promise, but even there the promise
was somewhat illusory, for imperial European nations and an expanding
American republic were not seriously inclined to support or permit the
flourishing of black nationhood. These countries still had too great a
stake in human bondage.

For most of the 19th century Haiti still beckoned to black Americans, and African-American emigrants occasionally sought to reach it.
Haiti was an inspiration. As the century advanced, the promise of Haiti
seemed less justified, though not until the 20th century did it come to
seem completely unfounded.

In the United States, meanwhile, slavery seized a new lease on life.
Southern states developed a "Cotton Kingdom" and tobacco, sugar, and
rice diminished to local importance. King Cotton demanded black slaves
and produced a generation born into servitude. Unlike their immigrant
forefathers, these people had no memory of an African homeland and
depended upon stories handed down around fireplaces, campfires, and
bedsides for their knowledge of the ancestors. They might hear of their
people who had fought with the British, or against them, who had gone
overseas or run away and formed communities of their own. They would
have few opportunities for such heroics in the 19th century, although
heroics were never lacking. They might also hear of people who had
merely stayed and endured.

African Americans would have need of all their heroism and endur-
ance, for never did slavery come closer to a deadening uniformity nor
did concepts of white supremacy have greater currency than in the first
half of the 19th century, particularly after 1830. They would struggle to
maintain their integrity and self-worth and they would create a vibrant

and influential culture, one that intersected with and modified the dominant culture. They would nurse a tradition of forcible opposition to tyranny even when white Americans imposed a tyranny of their own.

Those blacks who gained their freedom faced their own ordeal. Northern free states believed as firmly in black inferiority as Southern slave states did. The idea that men of Washington and Jefferson's generation could have had any notion of including black people within the purview of their egalitarian statements became, for many white people, inconceivable by the 1830s and 1840s. If Northerners remembered the existence of slavery in their states at all, they would most likely explain its demise by reference to climate and economics rather than to the rights of man. The thought that black and white people could fight and vote and go to school together became a concept they could not sustain, and where states continued to provide blacks privileges as a heritage from the early days of revolution, white citizens moved to withdraw them. In vain might black revolutionary veterans recall their deeds of service to the country; in vain might black students quote the Declaration of Independence. In vain might black people advance a claim to their own pursuit of happiness. Only among a small group of militant abolitionists did this egalitarian tradition make much sense in relation to the blacks in their midst.

As they greeted the 19th century, most people, black and white alike, probably had little idea how far the nation would stray from the ideals expressed a quarter-century earlier. Most black people would have been deeply depressed to reflect that they had more than 60 years of bondage yet to survive. Most white people would have been greatly shocked to suspect how much they still had to pay for a national union based upon freedom and equality. The foundation for this union had already been laid, but the framework was not complete.

CHRONOLOGY

◇ ◇ ◇

1772

Somerset decision puts slavery on the road to extinction in England.

1773

African-born Phillis Wheatley publishes *Poems on Various Subjects, Religious and Moral* in England.

1775

Adam Smith's *The Wealth of Nations* casts doubt on the economic efficiency of slavery.

1775

Governor Lord Dunmore of Virginia issues a proclamation offering freedom to slaves of rebels who will fight together with the British.

1775

One of the first independent black Baptist congregations develops in Silver Bluff, South Carolina.

1776

American Declaration of Independence proclaims that all men are created equal.

1777

Blacks in Massachusetts and New Hampshire petition for freedom based upon principles of the Declaration of Independence.

1778

Black businessman Paul Cuffe and his brother John refuse to pay taxes, claiming taxation without representation.

1780

Pennsylvania enacts first gradual emancipation law.

1780

Blacks in Newport, Rhode Island, form the first Free African Union Society.

1783

Massachusetts outlaws slavery by court decision in the Quok Walker case.

1784

Death of Phillis Wheatley, poverty-stricken, in Boston at age 31.

1786

Black Poor Committee formed in London to aid needy African-American immigrants.

1787

British abolitionists found the Society for the Abolition of the Slave Trade.

1787

British reformers establish the colony of Sierra Leone to receive black American immigrants in London and other freed slaves.

1787

American Constitutional Convention develops a new government protecting slavery.

1787

Northwest Ordinance forbids slavery in American territory north of the Ohio river and east of the Mississippi.

1787

Richard Allen and Absalom Jones form the Free African Society in Philadelphia.

1788

French abolitionists found the Society of the Friends of the Blacks.

1788

Massachusetts prohibits all foreign blacks, except those from Morocco, from living in the state for more than two months.

1789

French Declaration of the Rights of Man and Citizen proclaims equal rights for all.

1790

Charleston's free black people organize the Brown Fellowship Society.

1791

Haitian revolution begins.

1793

Eli Whitney's cotton gin spurs economic expansion and tightens the bonds of slavery.

1793

Blacks volunteer their services during a yellow fever epidemic in Philadelphia.

1794

Abolition of slavery in the French Empire.

1794

The St. Thomas African Episcopal Church of Philadelphia opens its doors.

1794

Richard Allen establishes Bethel African Methodist church in Philadelphia.

1798

Toussaint Louverture expels the British and becomes the most powerful leader in French colony of Saint Domingue.

1799

New York's manumission law frees the children of slaves born after July 4.

1800

Gabriel's conspiracy in Virginia

1802

Napoleon reinstitutes slavery in the French Empire.

1802

Toussaint Louverture betrayed and imprisoned in France.

1804

New Jersey becomes the last Northern state to pass a manumission act.

1804

Haiti becomes an independent nation.

FURTHER READING

◇ ◇ ◇

GENERAL AFRICAN-AMERICAN HISTORY

Bennett, Lerone, Jr. *Before the Mayflower: A History of Black America.* 6th rev. ed. New York: Viking Penguin, 1988.

———. *The Shaping of Black America.* New York: Viking Penguin, 1993.

Blackburn, Robin. *The Overthrow of Colonial Slavery, 1776–1848.* New York: Verso, 1988.

Foner, Philip S. *History of Black Americans: From Africa to the Emergence of the Cotton Kingdom.* Westport, Conn.: Greenwood, 1975.

Franklin, John H., and Alfred A. Moss, Jr. *From Slavery to Freedom: A History of Negro Americans.* 7th ed. New York: Knopf, 1994.

Gates, Henry L., Jr. *A Chronology of African-American History from 1445–1980.* New York: Amistad, 1980.

Genovese, Eugene. *From Rebellion to Revolution: Afro-American Slave Revolts in the Making of the Atlantic World.* Baton Rouge: Louisiana State University Press, 1979.

Giddings, Paula. *When and Where I Enter: The Impact of Black Women on Race and Sex in America.* New York: Bantam, 1985.

Harding, Vincent. *There Is a River: The Black Struggle for Freedom in America.* San Diego: Harcourt Brace, 1981.

Hine, Darlene C., et al., eds. *Black Women in America.* Brooklyn, N.Y.: Carlson, 1993.

Litwack, Leon, and Meier, August. *Black Leaders of the 19th Century.* Urbana: University of Illinois Press, 1988.

McCloy, Shelby T. *The Negro in the French West Indies.* Lexington: University of Kentucky Press, 1966.

Meltzer, Milton. *The Black Americans: A History in Their Own Words.* Rev. ed. New York: HarperCollins, 1984.

Mintz, Sidney W., and Richard Price. *The Birth of African-American Culture: An Anthropological Perspective.* Boston: Beacon Press, 1992.

Quarles, Benjamin. *The Negro in the Making of America.* 3rd ed. New York: Macmillan, 1987.

Rice, C. Duncan. *The Rise and Fall of Black Slavery.* Baton Rouge: Louisiana State University Press, 1975.

THE AMERICAN REVOLUTION

Berlin, Ira, and Ronald Hoffman, eds. *Slavery and Freedom in the Age of the American Revolution.* Charlottesville: University Press of Virginia, 1983.

Davis, David B. *The Problem of Slavery in the Age of Revolution, 1770–1823.* Ithaca: Cornell University Press, 1975.

Flexner, James T. *George Washington: Anguish and Farewell (1793–1799).* Boston: Little, Brown, 1972.

———. *George Washington in the American Revolution (1775–1783).* Boston: Little, Brown, 1968.

Frey, Sylvia R. *Water from the Rock: Black Resistance in a Revolutionary Age.* Princeton, N.J.: Princeton University Press, 1991.

Greene, Jack P. *All Men are Created Equal: Some Reflections on the Character of the American Revolution.* Oxford: Clarendon Press, 1976.

Kaplan, Sidney, and Emma Nogrady Kaplan. *The Black Presence in the Era of the American Revolution.* Amherst: University of Massachusetts Press, 1989.

Morgan, Edmund. *The Birth of the Republic, 1763–89.* Chicago: University of Chicago Press, 1992.

Nash, Gary. *Race and Revolution.* Madison, Wis.: Madison House, 1990.

Quarles, Benjamin. *The Negro in the American Revolution.* Chapel Hill: University of North Carolina Press, 1961.

Wood, Gordon. *The Creation of the American Republic, 1776–1787.* Chapel Hill: University of North Carolina Press, 1969.

REVOLUTION IN FRANCE AND HAITI

Cole, Hubert. *Christophe: King of Haiti.* London: Eyre & Spottiswoode, 1967.

Fick, Carolyn E. *The Making of Haiti: The Saint Domingue Revolution from Below.* Knoxville: University of Tennessee Press, 1990.

Geggus, David P. *Slavery, War, and Revolution: The British Occupation of Saint Domingue, 1793–1798.* Oxford: Clarendon Press, 1982.

Hunt, Alfred N. *Haiti's Influence on Antebellum America: Slumbering Volcano in the Caribbean.* Baton Rouge: Louisiana State University Press, 1988.

James, C. L. R. *The Black Jacobins: Toussaint L'Ouverture and the San Domingo Revolution.* Revised ed. London: Allison & Busby, 1980.

Korngold, Ralph. *Citizen Toussaint: A Biography.* New York: Hill and Wang, 1965.

Logan, Rayford W. *The Diplomatic Relations of the United States with Haiti, 1776–1891.* Chapel Hill: University of North Carolina Press, 1941.

Ott, Thomas O. *The Haitian Revolution, 1789–1804.* Knoxville: University of Tennessee Press, 1973.

Rude, George. *Revolutionary Europe, 1783–1815.* New York: Harper Torchbooks, 1964.

AFRICAN-AMERICAN CULTURE AND SOCIETY

Andrews, William L. *To Tell a Free Story: The First Century of Afro-American Autobiography, 1760–1865.* Urbana: University of Illinois Press, 1986.

Berlin, Ira. *Slaves without Masters: The Free Negro in the Antebellum South.* New York: Oxford University Press, 1974.

Chaplin, Joyce E. *An Anxious Pursuit: Agricultural Innovation and Modernity in the Lower South, 1730–1815.* Chapel Hill: University of North Carolina Press, 1993.

Egerton, Douglas R. *Gabriel's Rebellion: The Virginia Slave Conspiracies of 1800 and 1802.* Chapel Hill: University of North Carolina Press, 1993.

Fitts, Leroy. *A History of Black Baptists.* Nashville, Tenn.: Broadman Press, 1984.

———, and Charles T. Davis. *The Slave's Narrative.* New York: Oxford University Press, 1985.

Gewehr, Wesley M. *The Great Awakening in Virginia, 1740–1790.* Gloucester, Mass.: Peter Smith, 1965.

Hatch, Nathan O. *The Democratization of American Christianity.* New Haven: Yale University Press, 1989.

Jordan, Winthrop D. *White over Black: American Attitudes toward the Negro, 1550–1812.* Chapel Hill: University of North Carolina Press, 1968.

Littlefield, Daniel C. *Rice and Slaves: Ethnicity and the Slave Trade in Colonial South Carolina.* Baton Rouge: Louisiana State University Press, 1981.

Miller, Floyd J. *The Search for a Black Nationality: Black Colonization and Emigration, 1787–1863*. Urbana: University of Illinois Press, 1975.

Morton, Louis. *Robert Carter of Nomini Hall: A Virginia Tobacco Planter of the Eighteenth Century*. Charlottesville: University Press of Virginia, 1941.

Mullin, Gerald W. *Flight and Rebellion: Slave Resistance in Eighteenth-Century Virginia*. New York: Oxford University Press, 1972.

Nash, Gary B. *Forging Freedom: The Formation of Philadelphia's Black Community, 1720–1840*. Cambridge: Harvard University Press, 1988.

Nell, William C. *The Colored Patriots of the American Revolution*. 1855. Reprint, Salem, N.H.: Ayer Publishers, 1986.

Payne, Daniel A. *History of the African Methodist Episcopal Church*. 1891. Reprint, New York: Arno Press, 1969.

Porter, Dorothy, ed. *Early Negro Writing, 1760–1837*. Boston: Beacon Press, 1971.

———. *Negro Protest Pamphlets: A Compendium*. New York: Arno Press, 1969.

Raboteau, Albert J. *Slave Religion: The "Invisible Institution" in the Antebellum South*. New York: Oxford University Press, 1978.

Robinson, William H. *Black New England Letters: The Uses of Writings in Black New England*. Boston: Trustees of the Public Library, 1977.

———. *Early Black American Prose: Selections with Biographical Introductions*. Dubuque, Iowa: William C. Brown, 1971.

Ruchames, Louis. *Racial Thought in America: A Documentary History. Volume I: From the Puritans to Abraham Lincoln*. Amherst: University of Massachusetts Press, 1969.

Sernett, Milton C. *Black Religion and American Evangelicalism: White Protestants, Plantation Missions, and the Flowering of Negro Christianity, 1787–1865*. Metuchen, N.J.: Scarecrow Press, 1975.

Simms, James M. *The First Colored Baptist Church in North America. Constituted at Savannah, Georgia, January 20, A.D. 1788*. 1888. Reprint, New York: Negro Universities Press, 1969.

Smith, Charles S. *A History of the African Methodist Episcopal Church*. New York: Johnson Reprint, 1968.

Sobel, Mechal. *Trabelin' On: The Slave Journey to an Afro–Baptist Faith*. Westport, Conn.: Greenwood Press, 1979.

Stuckey, Sterling. *Slave Culture: Nationalist Theory and the Foundations of Black America*. New York: Oxford University Press, 1987.

Walls, William J. *The African Methodist Episcopal Zion Church: Reality of the Black Church*. Charlotte, N.C.: A.M.E. Zion Publishing House, 1974.

Wilmore, Gayraud S. *Black Religion and Black Radicalism: An Interpretation of the Religious History of Afro-American People*. 2nd ed., revised and enlarged. Maryknoll, N.Y.: Orbis, 1983.

Wood, Gordon S. *The Radicalism of the American Revolution*. New York: Knopf, 1992.

SLAVERY AND THE BRITISH EMPIRE

Drescher, Seymour. *Capitalism and Antislavery: British Mobilization in Comparative Perspective*. New York: Oxford University Press, 1987.

Fyfe, Christopher. *A History of Sierra Leone*. London: Oxford University Press, 1962.

Porter, Dale H. *The Abolition of the Slave Trade in England, 1784–1807*. New York: Archon Books, 1970.

Wilson, Ellen Gibson. *The Loyal Blacks*. New York: G. P. Putnam, 1976.

Winks, Robin W. *The Blacks in Canada: A History*. New Haven: Yale University Press, 1971.

BIOGRAPHIES

Bedini, Silvio A. *The Life of Benjamin Banneker*. New York: Scribners, 1972.

Conley, Kevin. *Benjamin Banneker*. New York: Chelsea House, 1989.

Crawford, George W. *Prince Hall and His Followers. Being a Monograph on the Legitimacy of Negro Masonry*. 1914. Reprint, New York: AMS Press, 1971.

Diamond, Arthur. *Paul Cuffe*. New York: Chelsea House, 1989.

———. *Prince Hall*. New York: Chelsea House, 1991.

George, Carol V. R. *Segregated Sabbaths: Richard Allen and the Rise of Independent Black Churches, 1760–1840*. New York: Oxford University Press, 1973.

Hodges, Graham. *Black Itinerants of the Gospel: The Narratives of John Jea and George White*. Madison, Wis.: Madison House, 1993.

Klots, Steve. *Richard Allen*. New York, Chelsea House, 1990.

Richmond, Merle. *Phillis Wheatley*. New York: Chelsea House, 1988.

Robinson, William H. *Phillis Wheatley and Her Writings*. New York: Garland, 1984.

Thomas, Lamont D. *Rise to Be a People: A Biography of Paul Cuffe*. Urbana: University of Illinois Press, 1986.

INDEX

◇ ◇ ◇

ACKNOWLEDGMENTS

◇ ◇ ◇

This volume owes a particular debt to the work of several historians: Sylvia Frey's *Water from the Rock*, covering the Revolutionary War in the South; Shane White's *Somewhat More Independent*, on emancipation in New York; and Gary Nash's *Forging Freedom*, on blacks in Philadelphia, were particularly helpful on their topics. My mentor Jack P. Greene's "'Slavery or Independence': Some Reflections on the Relationship among Liberty, Black Bondage, and Equality in Revolutionary South Carolina" in *South Carolina Historical Magazine* 80 (1979): 193-214; Joyce Chaplin's *An Anxious Pursuit*, on economic change in South Carolina; and Graham Hodges's *Black Itinerants of the Gospel* were also quite helpful. Sidney and Emma Kaplan's illustrated work on blacks in the Revolutionary War was both useful and inspirational. In singling out these people I do not intend to slight the work of others listed in the Further Reading, on whose work I also drew.

I wish to thank Deborah Gray White for suggesting me for this project in the first place, and Earl Lewis, Robin Kelley, and Nancy Toff for their help along the way. I also wish to thank Arnita Althaus for her help in preparing the manuscript, and my colleague Paul Schroeder for his comments on my treatment of the French Revolution.

I dedicate this book to my wife, Valinda W. Littlefield, whose intellectual curiosity, emotional support, and unfailing good cheer make life worth living.

PICTURE CREDITS

◇ ◇ ◇

DANIEL C. LITTLEFIELD

◇ ◇ ◇

Daniel C. Littlefield is professor of history and African-American studies at the University of Illinois, Urbana/Champaign. He is the author of *Rice and Slaves: Ethnicity and the Slave Trade in Colonial South Carolina.*

ROBIN D.G. KELLEY

◇ ◇ ◇

Robin D. G. Kelley is professor of history and Africana studies at New York University. He previously taught history and African-American studies at the University of Michigan. He is the author of *Hammer and Hoe: Alabama Communists during the Great Depression,* which received the Eliot Rudwick Prize of the Organization of American Historians and was named Outstanding Book on Human Rights by the Gustavus Myers Center for the Study of Human Rights in the United States. Professor Kelley is also the author of *Race Rebels: Culture, Politics, and the Black Working Class* and co-editor of *Imagining Home: Class, Culture, and Nationalism in the African Diaspora.*

EARL LEWIS

◇ ◇ ◇

Earl Lewis is professor of history and Afroamerican studies at the University of Michigan. He served as director of the university's Center for Afroamerican and African Studies from 1990 to 1993. Professor Lewis is the author of *In Their Own Interests: Race, Class and Power in Twentieth Century Norfolk* and co-author of *Blacks in the Industrial Age: A Documentary History.*